Reform Can Make a Difference

A Guide to School Reform

Darlene Leiding

ROWMAN & LITTLEFIELD EDUCATION
Lanham • New York • Toronto • Plymouth, UK

Published in the United States of America
by Rowman & Littlefield Education
A Division of Rowman & Littlefield Publishers, Inc.
A wholly owned subsidiary of The Rowman & Littlefield Publishing Group, Inc.
4501 Forbes Boulevard, Suite 200, Lanham, Maryland 20706
www.rowmaneducation.com

Estover Road
Plymouth PL6 7PY
United Kingdom

British Library Cataloguing in Publication Information Available

Library of Congress Cataloging-in-Publication Data

Leiding, Darlene, 1943-
  Reform can make a difference : a guide to school reform / Darlene Leiding.
    p. cm.
  Includes bibliographical references.
  ISBN 978-1-60709-406-7 (cloth : alk. paper) — ISBN 978-1-60709-407-4 (pbk. :
alk. paper) — ISBN 978-1-60709-408-1 (electronic)
  1. Educational change—United States. 2. Public schools—United States. I. Title.
  LA217.2.L445 2009
  370'.973—dc22   2009020061

∞™ The paper used in this publication meets the minimum requirements of
American National Standard for Information Sciences—Permanence of
Paper for Printed Library Materials, ANSI/NISO Z39.48-1992.
Manufactured in the United States of America.

Contents

Introduction

The faithful witness . . . is at his/her best when he/she concentrates on questioning and avoids the specialist's obsession with solutions.

—Saul, *Voltaire's Bastards*, 1992

One day in late spring, an envelope arrives in the mail from your son's middle school. Inside is his report card: an A, two Bs, a C, a D, and an F. Next to each grade is a brief comment from most, but not all, of his teachers. "Could do better," "excellent book report," "lacks initiative."

What are you to make of this report card? Is he a good student, a mediocre one, or teetering on the verge of failure? The report card is useless in helping you make that judgment. The grades are meaningless since the teachers have not made clear what standards underlie them. The report card itself is too late to correct the problems in the math class where he received the F or the science class where he received the D. Meanwhile, he gets promoted to eighth grade without any assurances that he actually mastered the material in seventh grade.

You make an appointment to speak with the teacher. He explains to you that in the course of an average day he has very little time to give individual students the help they need. He spends most of his time teaching the class, collecting permission slips, herding the class to assemblies, standing guard in the cafeteria at lunchtime, and trying to manage the students who are disruptive in class. At night the teacher stays up late preparing the next day's lesson plans to make the most of his teaching time. He is frustrated and exhausted. He says he finds your child likeable and compliant, but he simply does not have enough time to fully diagnose and work with him on his weaknesses, much less help him develop his strengths.

1

Now, let's say that you become so motivated to improve education that you decide to make a difference and make changes and run for your local school board. You want to advocate for reform, for change. You spend the next three months meeting voters, speaking at debates, sending out mailings, and shaking hands. To your surprise, you win! You now find yourself on a school board that is dealing with a $20 million budget, a defensive teacher's union, scared administration, litigious parents, and tough new federal and state standards. The board itself spends more time deliberating brick-and-mortar and administrative decisions than reforming education.

The effects of inadequate instruction are not felt merely by individuals, but also by the country as a whole. There are far too many young people leaving school unprepared for college, work, parenthood, and citizenship. Education is not neutral. It is political, ideological, social, and involves some form of adult imposition. We are endowed with the responsibility of overseeing the education of America's children.

Numerous efforts at reform have made little dent in the problem, largely because people are addressing symptoms rather than root causes. We can do better. We can pinpoint problems and provide effective solutions.

What does it mean to be well educated? No one should offer pronouncements about what it means to be well educated without meeting my friend Keith. When I met him, he was at the University of California, Los Angeles putting the finishing touches on his doctoral dissertation in molecular biology. A year later, after spending his entire life in school, he decided to apply to medical school. Today he is a practicing doctor and very successful judging by feedback from his patients and colleagues.

However, if I ask Keith what nine times seven is, he freezes, because he never learned his multiplication tables. Forget about grammar ("Me and her went to lunch.") or "Who is Steinbeck?" I am continuously amazed by the agility of Keith's mind as well as how much he does not know.

So, what do you make of this paradox? Is Keith a walking indictment of an educational system that let him get so far, years and years of schooling, graduate school, and medical school, without acquiring the basics of English and math? Or do we need to rethink what it means to be well educated, since what Keith lacks has not prevented him from being a deep-thinking, high-functioning, multicredentialed, professionally successful individual?

Of course, if those features describe what it means to be well educated, then there is no dilemma to be solved. Keith fits the bill. The problem arises only if your definition includes a list of facts and skills that one must have, but that Keith lacks. I have come to realize just how many truly brilliant people cannot spell or punctuate. Their insights and discoveries may be changing the shapes of their respective fields, but they can't use an apostrophe or comma correctly to save their lives.

Maybe we each should ask, "How well educated am I?" Does the phrase well educated refer to the quality of the schooling you received or something about the inner you? Does it denote what you were taught or what you learned and remember?

Every child is born with a desire to learn. A child's mind is hungry for knowledge, stimulation, and the excitement of exploring and learning. Indeed, most children enter kindergarten excited about learning to read and write and eager to know about the world around them. Yet, by the time they reach middle school (and often before), many look at learning as drudgery, not the exciting opportunity that propelled them when they were little. I have seen this firsthand in my travels around the country. In almost all of the schools I have visited I have found children in grade 3 eager and anxious to learn. By the time they are in eighth grade, they can take it or leave it. When they finally get to high school, I get the feeling that students would rather be anyplace except in school. Many avoid school like the plague.

A child's school should provide students with the desire to learn, but most do not. From kindergarten through high school, our public educational system is among the worst in the developed world. Instead of preparing our children for the highly competitive, information-based economy in which we now live, our school practices have severely curtailed their ability and desire to learn.

Failure or success in middle and high school is crucial to the nation's future. If a culture is to prosper, its adolescents must receive a more than mediocre secondary education. They need an education that prepares them for life.

There is a solution. Reform our schools so that our primary mission is to make school a place where students do not simply "put in time" but one where they will invest time and effort solving problems they see as relevant and want to solve and their enthusiasm for school will grow, their test scores will rise, and they will become successful citizens in our Information Age economy. Living and learning and teaching have to occur everywhere. We need to blur the distinctions between school life and real life. We must answer old questions as well as answer new ones.

From the president of the United States to the president of the local parent-teacher association, everyone is talking about schools. More than ever before, people recognize the value of a quality education for all Americans. The demand for well-educated, highly skilled workers is growing.

Education provides more than skills for careers. It teaches self-discipline, creativity, and patience. It prepares people to cope with change. It is invaluable for citizens who must understand and deal with complex social and political issues in a democratic society.

However, there is evidence that education is suffering from a lack of attention and support. Have Americans lost sight of the discipline and high expectations needed to obtain a solid education? Parents are citing concerns about low funding, poor discipline, violence, gangs, and drug abuse. Colleges and universities complain bitterly that professors are now forced to add remedial courses to teach incoming freshmen how to write simple sentences and compute basic mathematical formulas. Businesspeople, too, are frustrated by secretaries who cannot spell or write a business letter and by machine operators who do not read well enough to understand operating instructions.

People wonder why the United States, a country known for its creativity and drive, has not found solutions to the troubles that plague the nation's schools.

With all the very recent talk and attention now being given to education, change is on the horizon. Troubled schools must be improved. Schools need to adopt new techniques and new technology in order to meet higher academic expectations. Educators should be flexible and creative as they deal with issues surrounding curriculum, teacher training, funding, school choice, and a host of social problems. We need a drastic overhaul in education so that all students have new and better opportunities. Change is difficult, but change we must have.

Because Americans have so many different expectations for education, it is sometimes difficult to determine just how well schools are doing today. Certain undesirable qualities have been defined, but few schools are troubled by all of them, just as few schools are problem free. Most schools can be said to do an adequate job in some areas and a less than adequate job in others. For instance, a school might have talented teachers but poor administration or an excellent curriculum but overcrowded facilities.

In spite of the difficulties, there are several common standards by which some people judge schools. The first standard is the success of students: how many graduate, find careers, contribute to the community, and act as responsible citizens. Considering the millions of young people who are successful, a great number of schools must be doing an adequate job of educating. On the other hand, dropout rates, unemployment, and rising crime seem to show that a significant number of schools fall short of achieving acceptable results.

Bureaucracy, layers of administration operating under inflexible rules and regulations, is an enemy of larger school districts. Over time dozens of administrative offices and programs have been formed to deal with issues such as security, dropout prevention, and testing. While some programs are useful and necessary, carelessness, waste, and dishonesty are common. Change is difficult. Time and money continually drain resources away from the primary goal, the education of students.

Teachers also make a difference in how well a school educates or fails to educate its students. We must allow teachers to have freedom to express themselves, to improvise, and to manage discipline. We should even allow an unconventional approach to teaching.

Parents are a huge part of helping schools succeed. When parents are interested and involved in education, they show commitment to schools. Children from fragmented families or families that do not recognize the benefits of education are at an increased risk of failure in schools today. There is no one at home after school to praise a child for doing well or to listen to a problem. Time for these children is passed on the street with friends.

Communities can be supportive. Without strong support, schools can become settings for violence and crime. Gangs take the place of families. Although problems with drugs, guns, and gangs are not new challenges for Americans, they cause an increasing number of problems in schools today. "If you have the money, you can get yourself a 'tool' in fifteen minutes," one of my students told me. "Most of the kids here have guns or can easily get them."

This problem is no longer limited to inner-city schools either. In small towns and middle-class communities across the nation violence is disrupting education. I remember reading about an incident in Ballard, Washington, a couple of years ago. Sixteen-year-old Melissa Fernandez was fatally wounded when a carload of gang-affiliated teens drove past and fired randomly as she was walking home from school. Education alone can do little to stem this violence, which usually begins on the streets and spills over to school grounds, but we must try.

In a fast-changing world where school violence is a growing concern, where standardized tests are applied as simplistic "quick fixes," where rapid advances in science and technology threaten to outpace schools' effectiveness, where the average tenure of a school district superintendent is less than three years, and where students, parents, and teachers feel weighted down by increasing pressures, this book on school reform offers much-needed material for the dialogue about educating our children.

For the past hundred years, Americans have argued and worried about the quality of their schools. Some have charged that students are not learning enough, while others have complained that the schools are not at the forefront of social progress.

There are countless accounts of grandiose efforts by educational reformers to use the schools to promote social and political goals, even when they diminished the schools' ability to educate children. Generations of reformers have engaged in social engineering, advocating for industrial education, intelligence testing, curriculum differentiation, and life-adjustment education. These reformers mounted vigorous campaigns against academic studies.

American schools appear to have been damaged by three misconceptions. The first is the belief that schools can solve any social or political problem. The second is the belief that only a portion of teens is capable of benefiting from high-quality education. The third is that imparting knowledge is relatively unimportant compared to engaging students in activities and experiences. These errors have restricted equality of educational opportunity. Academic standards have been lowered. They have produced a diluted and bloated curriculum and pressure to enlarge schools so they can offer multiple tracks to students with different occupational goals. As a result the American high school is too big, too anonymous, and lacks instructional coherence. We seem to have lost track of the concept that all students have the capacity to learn and all are equally deserving of a solid education.

Mayor Bloomberg, New York City, in a report published May 15, 2007, said that as he continues to fight for improvement and reform in New York's public schools there must be an overhaul of the entire educational system, the "school swamp," singling out "the dominant culture of funded failure that corrupts the entire system." He reported that everyone in the system knows this sad, unspoken secret: the poorer the performance of the students, the larger the payroll. Failure is funded. Success is ignored. There are no countervailing incentives for improved performance by teachers, administrators, or students.

The impact on the teaching corps in poor-performing schools is obvious. Newer and younger teachers have a very high attrition rate. Assigned to schools no other teacher chooses to go to, surrounded by teachers as new and inexperienced as themselves, younger teachers tend to have less support, less mentoring, and less success. A large percentage of younger teachers leave the field within three years.

Mayor Bloomberg also commented on how devastating this is for the students. They don't benefit from the wisdom and professionalism that years of trial and error can bring a teacher. Instead, the students see the newest and least equipped teachers year after year. The turnover is high and the morale and performance suffer.

The financial impact is also serious. Because the better schools have higher numbers of veteran teachers, they demand the bigger budgets. The poorly performing schools suffer even more.

The success of any city's most challenged schools depends not just on more funds but also on the gradual redistribution of more experienced teachers into every city school. Without a corps of veteran teachers, no amount of money can make students and schools succeed.

For most of the twentieth century, Americans have argued about their public schools, some claiming that they are not as good as they used to be, others say that they are not as good as they ought to be. Some think the schools should go back to basics; others insist that schools should break free of basics. Some want higher standards; others want schools where students pursue their own interests without any external pressures. Some think that schools must liberate themselves from the dead hand of tradition, others that schools are plagued by too many foolish reforms. Each generation supposes that its complaints are unprecedented. It is impossible to find a period in the twentieth century in which educational reformers, parents, and the citizenry were satisfied with the schools.

As we enter the twenty-first century, Americans want traditions that nourish and ideas that make sense of a world that is changing swiftly. One of the great virtues of academic tradition is that it organizes human knowledge and makes it comprehensible to the learner. It aims to make a chaotic world coherent. It gives intellectual strength to those who want to understand social experience and the nature of the physical world. Despite sustained efforts to diminish it, the academic tradition survives. It survives because knowledge builds on knowledge, and we cannot dispense with the study of knowledge without risking mass ignorance. It survives because it retains the power to enlighten and liberate those who seek knowledge. As parents, educators, policymakers, and reformers it is time for us to renew the academic tradition for the children of the twenty-first century.

How does the American educational system stack up worldwide? Take a young boy or girl from a typical (if there is such a thing) American family who goes to a typical American school, and imagine that child growing up in France, Germany, Japan, or Taiwan. Few would choose to make the experiment. Most Americans tend to believe that this country, with its tradition of political freedom and its generous optimism, is the greatest country in the world. But the evidence is strong that the very same young child would grow up much more competent in those other countries than in the United States. He or she would have learned much more in the earlier grades in those European or Asian countries. Although our political traditions and even our universities may be without peer, our K–12 education is among the least effective in the developed world. Its controlling theories, curricular incoherencies, and naturalistic fallacies are barriers to a successful education. Imagine what our children could become under a good, demanding, and fair educational system!

The disappointments of reform to date have not led educational experts to question the romantic principles on which their proposals are based, but rather to attack the messenger that is bringing the bad news, which some call standardized tests. Whatever the shortcomings of these tests, no one has plausibly denied that they show a positive correlation with academic competencies. No one has plausibly denied that the better one reads, the higher one tends to score on standardized reading tests. If reform efforts of the past decade were significantly improving our children's academic competencies, then the standardized tests, however imperfect, would yield some indication of it. We need to pick up ideas and clues to effective practices wherever we can find then. We should always take theories, use them, and then replace them with better ones.

There is a widening gap between rich and poor, and a correlation with a gap in educational achievement exists. Economic class currently determines educational attainment in U.S. schools more than race.

In this age of budget cutbacks, our public schools, just like charitable organizations, need the skills, goods, and contributions of everyone in the community. But when we think of giving we rarely think of schools, especially if we don't have children in them. Also, giving to schools is not quite as easy as writing a check in response to a disaster or fundraising appeal or volunteering to work at a soup kitchen or phone bank.

Reform must include involvement. There are many ways we can become involved in our schools. Some may take very little time, like donating a computer or thoughtfully voting for school board members or a budget. Others take more time, such as volunteering in the office, joining an advocacy group, or working on a school campaign. More time is required for some commitments, like mentoring a student, serving on a parent committee, or serving as a classroom aide. There is a lot to learn before you take the plunge. How did public education get to be the way it is? How is it organized? Where are the decisions made? Is reform really the answer?

America has rarely been satisfied with its schools. Every decade has had its share of school critics and educational reformers. The debate is getting more vociferous.

Schools are not doing well because they are forced to struggle against tough odds. Gun-toting students are just one of the horror stories we've been hearing about. Do you know how many different languages are spoken in your district schools? Not how many are taught, but how many children come to school unable to speak English? Parents may speak even less English, impeding their efforts to aid their children.

What shape are your school buildings in? A poor physical environment can defeat the efforts of even the most innovative and competent teachers.

You can make a difference. You can create a support system to help kids succeed (after-school tutoring, career advice, resources, cultural opportunities). You can encourage good citizenship through modeling service to others. You can vote; serve as a volunteer, classroom aide, or coach; and assist in countless other ways.

We have been fighting an uphill battle. For the past forty years we have been trying to up the ante in getting the latest innovations and policies into place. We started naively in the 1960s, pouring huge amounts of money into large-scale national curriculum efforts, open schools, individual instruction, and the like. It was assumed, but not planned for, that something was bound to come of it. We have never really recovered from the profound disappointment experienced when our expectations turned out to be so far removed from the realities of implementation. Indeed, the term implementation was not even used in the 1960s.

The world of innocent expectations came crashing down around 1970, when the first implementation studies surfaced. A period of stagnation, recovery, and regrouping followed during most of the 1970s. Educators, especially in the first part of the decade, had a crisis of confidence. Perhaps the educational system and its inhabitants are not open to or capable of change? Perhaps, worse still, education, even if it improved, could not make a difference given social class, family, and other societal conditions outside the purview of the educational sector?

As educators plugged away, a few glimmers of hope came through. By the end of the 1970s, the effective schools movement had accumulated some evidence, a growing ideology that schools can make a difference even under trying conditions. On another front, intensive work on in-service and staff development by Bruce Joyce and others demonstrated that ongoing competence-building strategies can work. By 1980 we knew a fair amount about major factions associated with introducing innovations in education.

From a societal point of view this was too little, too late. As problems in society worsened, the educational system was tinkering with change. Even its so-called successes were isolated, and were the exception rather than the rule. Nothing was related to greater student learning.

By the early 1980s, society had enough. By about 1983 (in fact, the date is precise and coincides with the release of *A Nation at Risk*), the solution was seen as requiring large-scale governmental action. Structural solutions through top-down regulations were introduced. In many states curriculum was specified and mandated. Competencies for students and teachers were detailed and tested, salaries of teachers (woefully low at the time) were raised, leadership competencies were introduced and tested, and training took place. We became engaged in large-scale tinkering with the system.

Overlapping these top-down regulatory efforts was another movement, which began after 1985. In the United States it goes under the name restructuring. Here the emphasis is on school-based management, enhanced roles for principals and teachers, and other decentralized components.

Currently we have a combination of centralists, who see greater top-down regulation, accountability, and control of the educational establishment as the answer, on one side of the spectrum. This side includes strategies such as local management of schools, which attempts to place more power in the hands of local interests outside the school. The other side is instructionists, who see greater control by school-based teachers and other educators as the basic solution.

For most of us, confusion seemed to be the state of mind in the early 1990s. The ante had been upped in that we were no longer considering particular innovations one at a time, but rather more comprehensive reforms. The ante was also upped in that the solution was seen as too important to leave to educators. The federal government and business interests were now the major players.

We must realize that we are all engaged in higher-stakes solutions with more to win but also more to lose. It does not seem to be a good time to wallow in confusion. Tinkering, after all, can be on a large or small scale, its main characteristic being "a clumsy attempt to mend something" (*Webster's New World Dictionary*, 2005).

We appear to have been fighting an ultimately fruitless uphill battle. The solution is not how to climb the hill of getting more innovations or reforms into the system. We need a different hill, so to speak. We need a new mindset about educational reform. We need a change.

On one hand, we have the constant and ever-expanding presence of educational innovation and reform. On the other hand, we have an educational system that is fundamentally conservative. The way that teachers are trained, the way that schools are organized, the way that the educational hierarchy operates, and the way that educators are treated by political decisionmakers result in a system that is more likely to retain the status quo than to change. When change is attempted under such circumstances, it results in defensiveness, superficiality, or short-lived pockets of success.

The answer does not lie in designing better reform strategies. No amount of sophistication in strategizing for particular innovations or policies will ever work. It is unrealistic to expect that introducing reforms one by one, even major ones, in a situation that is basically not organized to engage in change will do anything but give reform a bad name. You cannot have an educational environment in which change is continuously expected alongside a conservative system and expect anything but constant aggravation.

What will it take to make the educational system a learning organization, expert at dealing with change as a normal part of its work not just in relation to the latest policy, but as a way of life? We need new mindsets to help us manage the unknown.

We must also ask why it is important that education develop such a change capacity. One could respond at the abstract level that change is all around us. Education should be producing critical thinkers and problem solvers. However, these have become clichés. A deeper reason is that education has a moral purpose: to make a difference in the lives of students regardless of background and to help produce citizens who can live and work productively in increasingly dynamically complex societies. This is not new either. What is new is the realization that to do this puts teachers precisely in the business of continuous innovation and change. They are in the business of making improvements, and to make improvements in an ever-changing world is to contend with and manage the forces of change on an ongoing basis.

Society expects its citizens to be capable of proactively dealing with change throughout life, both individually as well as collaboratively. Education has the potential to contribute to this goal. Yet education, far from being a hotbed of teaching people to deal with change in basic ways, is just the opposite. To break through this impasse, educators must see themselves and be seen as experts in the dynamics of change. Educators, administrators, and teachers alike must become skilled change agents. If they do become change agents and put the students first, educators will make a difference in the lives of students from all backgrounds and cultures, and by doing so help produce greater capacity in society to cope with change.

This is one goal you cannot tinker with. You cannot vaguely or obliquely expect it to happen and you cannot hope to accomplish it by playing it safe. Change capacity must become explicit and reform will follow with its pursuit.

Productive educational reform is not the capacity to implement the latest policy, but rather is the ability to survive the vicissitudes of planned and unplanned change while growing and developing. Knowledge in the process of educational reform is the missing ingredient in attempts to bring about educational innovation.

Educators cannot do this task alone. Too much is already expected of them. Teachers' jobs are more complex than ever before. They must respond to the needs of a diverse and constantly changing student population, rapidly changing technology in the workplace, and demands for excellence from all segments of society. The global marketplace raises the stakes even higher in its performance demands on schools. Deteriorating social conditions continue to widen the awful gap between the haves and the have-nots. As Goodlad (1995) says, "Healthy nations have healthy schools" (p. 7), not the other way around.

The focus of change and reform must be on all agencies and their interrelationships. But let us not lose track of the fact that educators have a special obligation to help lead the way in partnership with others.

American education is in crisis. We all know it; we keep hearing it over and over. According to most critics, from the 1983 government report *A Nation at Risk* to the analysis of scholars to the commonly heard complaints of parents, the quality of education has deteriorated.

Debates concerning the reasons for the failure of education run the gamut. Many believe it is the educational system itself that is to blame. While some critics believe schools need more money, others believe teachers are not doing their jobs. Still others believe that reformers must go even further than addressing funding and teacher quality. Many argue for vast reforms to the entire structure of the public educational system, including reorganizing school management, decreasing the government's involve-ment in schools, and increasing involvement of parents and communities. One critic simply says, "We can't fix the system. We need radical change."

Then you will find many who say that it is the quality of the students, and not the system, that has deteriorated. These critics believe that changes in the family structure and society (increases in divorce, poverty, unem-ployment, violence, gangs, drugs, etc.) have caused children's lives to be-come increasingly unstable and insecure. This, in turn, has made it more difficult for children to learn. These children face monumental problems such as physical abuse and neglect, dropout rates, poor grades, substance abuse, and crime. A student from a poverty-stricken, abusive, single-parent home who arrives at school inadequately dressed and underfed will have difficulty concentrating on his/her studies, regardless of the caliber of the teacher, the school, or the curriculum.

This broad range of concerns reveals that there is no quick solution to the nation's educational problems. Perhaps this is why the crisis in educa-tion appears to be insurmountable, despite the number of studies written, speeches made, and programs created to address it. However, the crisis needs to be addressed. If something is not done, the number of unskilled workers will climb, as will the number of illiterate adults. Our ability to compete economically will be threatened and our students' ability to achieve personal success will be hindered.

When you think about it, there is a lot to criticize about our schools: the way conformity is valued over curiosity and enforced with rewards and punishments, the way children are forced to compete against one another, the way meaning so often takes a backseat to skills in the curriculum, the way students are prevented from designing their own learning, the way instruction (not to mention assessment) is standardized, and the way dif-ferent avenues of study are rarely integrated into the program. This is just a warm-up.

The trick about reform, when deciding what we really want, is to look beyond the surface and think past the short term. We must be sure schools meet the needs of the students who attend them instead of forcing children to adapt to the needs of the educational institution.

As we ponder reform initiatives we must ask several questions: What should all students know in the twenty-first century, and who should decide this? What do good schools, where all students learn, look like, and how do they involve parents? How do they motivate students and teachers to do their best? Should we organize schools around the four *c*'s (competency-based curriculum, core values, collaboration, and community)?

There are more questions: What kinds of classrooms do we need to con-struct? What sorts of teaching are most likely to produce results? What sorts of teaching could get in the way of the hoped-for results?

Once you have decided that schools should meet the developmental needs of the children who attend them instead of just forcing children to adapt to the needs of the institution, what implications does that have for the kind of education we offer to teenagers? Once you've decided you want students to take satisfaction from their own accomplishments rather than to become dependent on the approval of authority figures, how does that affect the way you respond to their successes? Once you are sure you'd like your kids to realize that the life of someone who lives in Kabul or Baghdad is worth no less than the life of someone from their own neighborhood, what does that do to your social studies curriculum or your approach to character education? There are whys worth pondering beneath all the hows.

Such questioning can take place as a national dialogue, a concerted and deliberate invitation for all of us to reflect on the purpose of education. But it also can take place in a school parking lot as two or three teachers linger for a few moments to chat about what the point is of having students read a certain book or discuss a particular current event. Private conversations are fine as long as they are about how to nourish our public schools.

This book will address all of the above issues. Chapter 1 covers the history of reform and how this converges to the system we have today. Chapters 2 and 3 speak to the change process and teachers as change agents coupled with the effects of school culture on the process of change leading to comprehensive school reform. Chapters 4, 5, and 6 talk about school reform models, reinventing the American high school, and how school choice plays a major role in school reform. Chapter 7 speaks to current issues in educational reform, including assessment and professional competencies, and raises the question of whether the school system is the fundamental cause of social problems that our society faces today. Chapter 8 analyzes the role of poverty in school reform and argues that poverty places severe limits on what can be accomplished through school reform efforts. Chapter 9 simply concludes that results matter. Schools are starting to make changes based on the economic, social, and technological demands for student success.

We live in a time of great educational crisis. We rank below many industrial nations in reading, writing, and math. The world's narcotic economy is based on our consumption of this commodity. If we didn't buy as many powdered dreams the business would collapse, and schools are an important sales outlet. Our teenage suicide rate is one of the highest in the world and many suicidal kids are rich kids, not poor. New marriages last less than five years. Something is wrong!

It is absurd to be part of a system that compels you to sit in confinement with people of exactly the same age and social class. It is absurd to move from cell to cell at the sound of a gong every day of your natural youth in an institution that allows you no privacy and even follows you into the sanctuary of your home demanding that you do its "homework." Let's face it, two institutions control our children's lives: television and schooling, in that order.

The children I teach are indifferent to the adult world, have little curiosity, and cannot concentrate for very long. They have a poor sense of the future and of how tomorrow is inextricably linked to today. They do not realize how the past has predestinated their own present in limiting their choices or shaping their values and lives.

The children I teach are cruel to each other and laugh at weakness. They are uneasy with intimacy or candor. They are materialistic, often following television mentors who offer everything in the world for sale.

The children I teach are dependent, passive, and timid in the presence of new challenges. This timidness is frequently masked by surface bravado, by anger, or by aggressiveness.

We need to believe that self-knowledge is a basis for true knowledge. We need to invent school experiences that help develop self-reliance and uniqueness. We must listen to new voices and new ideas. We have to demand that these new voices and new ideas will get a hearing. We need my ideas and we need yours.

1

Historical Waves of Reform

> Whoever controls the image and information of the past determines what
> and how future generations will think; whoever controls the information
> and images of the present determines how the same people will view the
> past.
>
> —George Orwell, *1984*

Over the past four centuries America's schools have changed, along with
reform efforts about what it means to be a well-educated American.

For wealthy American colonists first arriving from England in the early
1600s, Latin was the most important area of study. It was the scholarly
language of Europe, used in theology, medicine, science, and foreign cor-
respondence. Not everyone in the early American colonies was supposed
to learn Latin, just the upper classes, but almost everyone was expected to
read the Bible.

By 1647, the Puritans, a dominant religious group in Massachusetts, decreed that every town with fifty households must support someone to teach
children to read and write. Every town of one hundred households should
set up a grammar school to prepare youth for the university.

The Revolutionary War left many colonial schools deserted, damaged, or
destroyed. In the years that followed, not only were schools rebuilt, they
were also redesigned to suit the new democracy, the newly created United
States of America.

When Thomas Jefferson called for the creation of a publicly funded
school system, he was looking for a way to turn the vast range of new
Americans into citizens. Each generation has grappled in turn with how education should shape and be shaped by an evolving nation. Tax-supported

schools opened their doors and almost instantly reforms began. Schools had to respond to the new demands brought on by massive immigration, child labor laws, and the explosive growth of cities, all which fueled school attendance and transformed public education.

Education became critical for the kind of citizens the new republic needed. Reading books with different levels of difficulty were developed and published. Spelling was introduced.

By the 1830s and 1840s, European immigrants were moving into the American cities. Farmers were moving from rural areas to the cities, enticed by factory jobs and livable wages. Schools were reformed for the masses. Students were taught to memorize and recite, rarely to think for themselves.

The public school as we know it was born in the mid-nineteenth century. Its founders called it the "common" school. Common schools were funded by local property taxes, charged no tuition, were open to all white children, were governed by a local school committee, and were subject to a modest amount of state regulation.

By the 1840s, things were changing quickly. The Northeast was undergoing an industrial revolution. The number of cities in the region with a population of more than 10,000 increased from three in 1800 to fifty-two by 1850 (Bernard and Mondale, 2001). Textile production shot up. Canals and railroads crisscrossed the nation. Immigration swelled, bringing large numbers of Roman Catholics to a predominantly Protestant nation. These factors formed the necessary preconditions for the creation of public schools. The pace of change and the urgency of new social problems fostered the development of new institutions. Alarmed reformers adopted various approaches to problems of poverty and vice. As the people moved west, they brought with them traditions of the common schools of the Eastern cities.

The end of the nineteenth century saw explosive growth in American public schools. Expenditures rose from $69 million in 1870 to $147 million in 1890. Public school enrollment increased from 1 million in 1870 to 2.7 million in the same decade (Bernard and Mondale, 2001). The United States was providing more schooling to more children than any other nation on earth, thanks to the nineteenth-century movement for school reform.

As the nineteenth century drew to a close, Americans prided themselves on their free public schools. Most children attended school, and America felt a patriotic attachment to them. Unlike in Europe, which was burdened with rigid class barriers, in America it was believed that the public school could enable any child to rise above the most humble of origins and make good on the nation's promise of equal opportunity for all.

What was important was not learning a trade but learning knowledge and virtue. As children became more knowledgeable and broad-minded, the community would improve. This was the American dream: the promise of the public school to open wide the doors of opportunity to all who were willing to learn and study. The schools would work their democratic magic by disseminating knowledge to all who sought it.

America had begun with common schools that included grades one through eight. By 1890, 95 percent of children between ages five and thirteen were enrolled in school for at least a few months each year (Ravitch, 2000).

The common schools emphasized reading, writing, speaking, spelling, penmanship, grammar, arithmetic, patriotism, a clear moral code, and strict discipline, which was enforced when necessary by corporal punishment. The values they sought to instill were honesty, industry, patriotism, responsibility, respect for adults, and courtesy.

The aim of the common school was clear: to promote sufficient learning and self-discipline so that people in a democratic society could be good citizens, read the newspaper, get jobs, make their way in an individualistic and competitive society, and contribute to their community's well-being.

At the end of the nineteenth century, almost every community had an elementary school, but public high schools were sparse. As the economy changed from agrarian to industrial and commercial, the youth began to need more education. There was a significant gap between elementary schools and the colleges and universities. New courses were introduced (botany, zoology, geology, physics, algebra, geometry, and foreign languages). The high school was born.

Immediately came an educational debate. While white educators were struggling to define the program of the public high school, black educators were struggling to expand access to publicly supported elementary schools for black children. Only a third of black children in 1890 attended any school at all, and few had any access to high school (Cremin, 1961).

As white educators were debating whether the educational ladder should be open to all students, black educators were worrying about how to secure the very lowest rung of the ladder for black children and debated which educational strategy (industrial education or liberal education, or a combination of both) was likeliest to improve the prospects for blacks' advancement.

At the turn of the century, there were two paths American education could take. One was an academic curriculum that would have all high school students, not just the college-bound few, study history, literature, science, math, languages. The other was a differentiated curriculum, which divided students according to their likely future occupations, offering practical studies for the vast majority and an academic curriculum for a small minority. Reformers agreed that the new century required a new system of education, but could not agree on what that new education should be.

In the early 1900s, *new education* had come to mean manual training, industrial education, vocational education, commercial studies, domestic science, agricultural studies, and other occupational programs. Criticism began immediately. Business leaders wanted economy and efficiency in the schools, and progressive educators wanted school curriculum to be more closely aligned to the needs of society in the Industrial Age. The business community also wanted well-trained workers. Progressive educators wanted socially efficient schools that would serve society by training students for certain jobs.

The progressive movement sought to make the schools more practical and realistic. It sought to recognize that students learn in different ways and that the health of children is important and to commit to social welfare, not only academic studies. Progressives pressed the schools to adjust to the rapidly changing society and to cast aside outmoded assumptions, one of which was the idea that the academic curriculum was appropriate for all children. A bookish curriculum blocked social progress, and it was not fit for the hordes of immigrant children crowding into the urban schools. These children, the reformers said, needed training for jobs in the industrial economy, not algebra and literature.

Critics for educational change attacked the high school curriculum as rigid and elitist. They heaped scorn on history, foreign language, and literature. They wanted a practical curriculum for those who would soon enter the workforce, especially those students who were poor, foreign-born, and nonwhite.

The arrival of millions of new immigrants between 1900 and 1920 had a large impact on the nation's schools. The majority of students in most large cities were either immigrants or children of immigrants. Many of these children came from desperately poor families and lived in crowded, malodorous slums, where public services were meager or nonexistent. Many schools during this era introduced medical and dental clinics in the facilities, evening and summer classes, vocational courses, and special classes for the physically and mentally handicapped.

During the first twenty years of the twentieth century, reformers debated several issues, including romantic pedagogy versus academic crusading for social efficiency, which would lead to educating as many children as possible to ensure improvement of society. This was based on student intelligence and character and encouraging the industrial education movement.

The 1920s brought about the age of experts. Reformers said that the objective of modern education is to socialize the students. Students should work in groups, not alone. In addition, there must be a shift in educational authority from parents, teachers, and school administrators to scientific experts in the new theory of education. Experts urged schools to divide up students into appropriate programs and groups. Education should be determined by the child's future occupation. Get rid of the old way of thinking in which equal opportunity meant that all children should have access to the same quality of education, and replace it with the new way of thinking in which equal opportunity meant that a banker's child would get a different education from a coal miner's child, and all would be fitted to occupy the status of their parents.

Instead of a ladder that stretched from kindergarten to the university and was open to all students, there would be many paths leading to different destinations: the future professional would prepare for college, the future farmer would study agriculture, the future housewife would study household management, the future clerk would study commercial subjects, the future industrial worker would study metalworking or woodworking, and so on.

Spurred by the endorsement of the experts, curricular differentiation spread rapidly into the public schools. Educational institutions moved from four curricular subjects to giving students a choice of forty-eight subjects.

It was during this time frame that surveys were introduced. Civic-minded citizens and business leaders closely scrutinized the efficiency and cost-effectiveness of their public schools. Critics were placated by surveys directed by efficiency experts. Between 1911 and 1930 nearly two hundred cities and states were surveyed by experts from major schools of education: Clebberley of Stanford, Strayer of New York Teachers College, Bobbitt of the University of Chicago, Elliott of the University of Wisconsin, and Hanus of Harvard (Tyack and Hansot, 1982).

These experts, through surveys, determined that some districts had growth in spelling, others in math, and that several districts were offering useless (in the experts' minds) subjects. Some surveys showed that schools should offer more vocational education. Overall, the experts decreed that schools should fit children into predetermined roles in an unchanging social order. None seemed to think there was anything to be gained from teaching a love of literature or history to all students; none made a case for a broad, rich liberal education. None believed that all children should have the same opportunity for an intellectually stimulating education. Surveys had a static notion of both the individual capacity for development and society's needs. They did not see young people as curious or having imagination. They could not imagine a future in which men and women, by improving their skills and knowledge, could change their occupations, much less change society.

The new gospel of industrial education and curricular differentiation dealt a deadly blow to the aspirations of African Americans. A half-century removed from slavery, 90 percent still lived in the South, and rampant racial prejudice had left Southern blacks disenfranchised, ill-educated, and powerless to fight for their rights at the ballot box or in the courts. What African Americans did not need was an education that would fit them into their preordained roles in society and their likely destinations as domestic servants, farmhands, and blacksmiths.

The only sustained dissent against industrial education and curricular differentiation came from a few classicists who considered this a threat to the humanistic tradition of the schools.

The years following World War I were dominated by the educational psychologists, who believed that they were on the verge of a major scientific breakthrough, the ability to measure the human mind. During the war, they had developed group intelligence tests for the army that quickly assigned large numbers of recruits to different duties. After the war, they perfected these tests for the public schools, which used them for vocational guidance and to assign students to different curricula.

Mental testing was the focus of the scientific movement in education. Educational psychologists produced both achievement tests and intelligence tests. Achievement tests aimed to determine what students had learned in school, while intelligence tests claimed to test what students were capable of learning. One tested knowledge, which could be taught and learned, while the other tested mental power, which most psychologists believed to be innate, inherited, and relatively constant over time.

By the late 1920s, and throughout the 1930s, there were new psychological trends that made a significant impact on the nation's public schools. A curriculum revision movement got underway, concentrated in the urban cities. This movement launched two major initiatives: one to determine what children needed to know to function successfully in contemporary society, the other to develop methods to help them learn what they still needed to know. This approach to education used individualized instruction, group projects, creative activities, and motivation through students' interest to reach goals and produce knowledgeable and skilled students. Spelling, penmanship, phonics, grammar, and mathematics were reintroduced. The spontaneity of children and their interests were both means and ends. With the future of the nation hanging in the balance, educators began to reconstruct society.

When the country plunged into a grinding economic depression in 1929, educators urged the schools to take a leading role in planning and creating a new social order. They believed that they could remake society by remaking the schools. Child-centered education was integrated with social reform. Perceiving the academic curriculum as a symbol for a corrupt and dying social order, they advocated replacement of academic studies with projects, real-life problem solving, activities, and socially useful experiences.

The curriculum revision movement paved the way for the activity movement in elementary schools during the late 1930s. The activity movement was inspired by projects and the importance of activities initiated by children's interests. Each classroom had a reading corner and a "center of interest" where students could explore activities that interested them, such as building a house or city out of blocks or themes involving boats or pets. Children were encouraged to do the kind of work they could do best and to enjoy the kind of experience they liked best, as long as they did not interfere with others. The success or failure of the program depended on the quality and ingenuity of the teachers.

While the activity movement swept the elementary schools during the late 1930s, junior high and high schools were influenced by the curriculum integration movement, which simply extended the premises of the activity movement into the upper grades and replaced subject matter with student experiences, socially significant studies, and life situations.

At this point the term core curriculum was introduced into educational circles. Principals echoed conventional wisdom: the curriculum should be centered around basic areas of human activity and consider the needs and interests of the students. In addition there must be core fields of instruction adjusted to the needs and interests of individuals. Subject matter should apply to real life, and be society-centered as opposed to subject-centered. Grades, honor rolls, contests, and other forms of rivalry and competition were eliminated.

When confronted with the dilemma of black youth, who still faced bleak prospects in a society where racial discrimination and segregation were common, educators urged them to accept society as it was instead of agitating for social change.

World War II dominated the early 1940s, and the schools continued to focus on the development of each individual child and prepare students for citizenship. By the end of World War II, progressivism was the reigning ideology of American education. The educational leadership was optimistic even though public education suffered from critical shortages of qualified teachers (due to the war), overcrowded schools, and a backlog of deferred maintenance from the Depression and war years. Education for all American youth defined the role of the public school. The main purpose was to develop career guidance, test students for their abilities, and then direct them either to vocational training or to a college preparatory program. College entrance would no longer depend on students' credits and grades, but would be based on tests of students' aptitude and intelligence and the recommendations of the high school.

Life adjustment education made its debut in 1945 at a conference convened by the U.S. Office of Education to discuss vocational education. The conference expected that there would be massive youth unemployment when the troops returned from the war. The group quickly decided that the schools should prepare 20 percent of the young people for college and another 20 percent for skilled labor occupations. The remaining 60 percent would receive life adjustment education. This would include home and family living courses, vocational education, and guidance services. Life adjustment also deemphasized learning from books and academic subjects. Experts in this area advised that the teaching of mathematics, for example, should concentrate on practical problems such as consumer buying, installment buying, insurance, and home budgeting, while courses in algebra, geometry, trigonometry, and solid geometry should be strictly elective, available only to a carefully selected few.

Life adjustment education was based on the assumption that 60 percent of the nation's youth lacked the brains for either college or skilled labor. Harl R. Douglass, dean of the College of Education at the University of Colorado and a prominent advocate for the life adjustment movement, claimed that this group actually accounted for more than 60 percent of the nation's young people. This large majority, he argued, was destined to become unskilled or semiskilled workers or the wives of laborers, and they did not need an academic education. What they needed was a functional program emphasizing the problems of "home, shop, store, citizenship, health, and welfare" (Douglass, 1949, p. 3).

The first half of the twentieth century was a time of remarkable expansion for the American public school system. Schools were called upon to teach the skills and knowledge needed for participation in a democratic industrial society to a rapidly growing and diverse population. Almost all children attended elementary school in 1900. By 1950, about 80 percent of teenagers were enrolled in high school. The United States led the world in fulfilling the promise of universal access to schooling.

Yet even as school enrollment multiplied, questions continually arose about what to teach, whether to give the same kind of education to all children, and how to allocate educational opportunities among different groups of children. The debates centered on differing ideas about what sort of education a democratic society should offer its children.

Early in the century, public schools had opened up a world of promise for children who came off the steamships and out of factories and farms. In the decades that followed, schools offered some students job training and groomed others for future leadership. The legacy of the era from 1900 to 1950 was a system of mass education, but one that educated different groups differently. The goal for the next generation would be to ensure equal education for *all* of America's children.

America in 1950 was a fundamentally different nation, one that is difficult to comprehend and appreciate from our contemporary angle of vision. Society kept changing, therefore the schools needed to change too. The family and the community became weaker and the schools now needed to address what the family and community used to do. The 1950s brought forth reformers who felt the best way of addressing the social and economic problems of society was to change the curriculum so that students could solve those problems themselves (by studying social living, family life, and consumer education). The traditional curriculum of academia was now declared undemocratic. Schools in Battle Creek, Michigan, introduced a health program. Kingsport, Tennessee, totally abandoned its academic subjects and letter grades for social skills and substituted narrative reports for those letter grades. In Alameda County, California, a course in world history/world issues was dropped to make room for driver education. Minneapolis, Minnesota, public schools initiated a common learning program devoted to studying problems meaningful to youth and building "right" attitudes. Classical literature and history were dropped.

By mid-century, the public schools had become agencies dedicated to socializing students, teaching them proper attitudes and behaviors, and encouraging conformity to the norms of social life and the workplace. Even the U.S. Supreme Court decision *Brown v. Board of Education* in 1954 did not alter the curriculum.

Storm clouds erupted in 1955 when Rudolf Flesch's book *Why Johnny Can't Read* reached the national best-seller lists, where it remained for more than thirty weeks. Serialized in many newspapers, Flesch's book struck a nerve, especially among parents who were not convinced that the new curriculum was effective in teaching basic skills. The reading wars soon began. Flesch complained that reading was not being taught at all. His comments set off a national debate about literacy.

Most people had their own opinion about reading. Some wanted letter sounds that then blended into words. Others wanted whole words, not letters and sounds. This whole language, no phonics, debate continues on today.

To make matters worse, the Soviet Union launched *Sputnik*, the first space satellite, in October 1957. The press treated *Sputnik* as a major humiliation for the United States as well as a dangerous threat to the nation's security. *Sputnik* became an instant metaphor for the poor quality of U.S. high schools. Overnight a clamor arose for higher academic standards and greater attention to mathematics, science, and foreign languages.

At the same time that *Sputnik* was shaking up the world and educational policy in the United States another force was lurking in the background. Segregation was no longer acceptable.

Melba Pattillo Beals was one of the nine African American teenagers chosen in 1957 to integrate Little Rock, Arkansas's Central High School. While white teenage girls were listening to Buddy Holly's "Peggy Sue," Melba was escaping the hanging rope of a lynch mob, dodging lighted sticks of dynamite, and washing away burning acid sprayed into her eyes. She says that she will always be grateful to the men of the 101st Airborne, the elite "Screaming Eagles" that President Eisenhower sent to Little Rock to keep the doors of Central High open and allow the nine teenagers to complete a full day of classes. At the center of the controversy were nine African American teenagers who wanted nothing more than a better education (Beals, 1994).

The crusade for equal educational opportunity that began in Little Rock, Arkansas, spread across the nation, aiding various struggles for learning and self-improvement. In 1966, African American students in Detroit, Michigan, protested the failure of urban schools and demanded better educational opportunities. In 1968, Mexican American high school students in Crystal City, Texas, demanded bilingual education, more humane treatment from white teachers, and curriculum reforms that included the history and culture of Mexicans in the Southwest.

Throughout the 1960s, American society was shaken by seismic social, cultural, and political changes. The years were characterized by turmoil and cataclysmic events. President John F. Kennedy, his brother Senator Robert Kennedy, and civil rights leader Martin Luther King Jr. were assassinated. Reaction against the war in Vietnam provoked massive antiwar protests, a radical student movement, a counterculture youth movement, and violent clashes between radical student groups and the police.

At the same time, the struggle for black civil rights led to protest demonstrations, bloody encounters between civil rights activists and Southern police, racist murders, and devastating urban riots in many major American cities.

The nation's schools were at the center of many social upheavals of that era. The baby boomers came of age and the schools grew rapidly to accommodate the surge in enrollment. Ready or not, American schools were also confused with the necessity of educating black children from a wide variety of backgrounds. Confronted with violence, disciplinary problems, and even litigation, students were left to fend for themselves without adult guidance. Teachers facilitated; they did not teach.

Public schools responded to the torrent of criticism that washed over them in the late 1960s by embracing the open education movement. Never before had an educational reform movement risen to national prominence almost overnight, won the enthusiastic support of educational leaders, dominated the national discussion, and then disappeared within a few years.

An open school emphasized projects, activities, and student initiative. Students did not have to sit in classrooms but could gather to learn in the school's halls or corridors and anywhere in the surrounding community. Emotional learning was more prized than intellectual learning. Multiage groups and individualized instruction were typical and quickly became the norm.

In 1975, the state of the nation's schools became a national political issue. Test scores were dropping, enrollment was declining, and curriculum needed to change again. English became language arts, with more attention to social issues; math and science became critical subjects once again; and the values of self-restraint, self-discipline, and humility were encouraged.

By the early 1980s, there was a growing concern about the quality of the nation's schools. The assault on the academic curriculum in the late 1960s and 1970s had taken its toll. In 1980, the Gannett newspaper chain sent investigative reporters into several schools in nine states, where they discovered that academic credit was offered for courses such as cheerleading, student government, and mass media.

In California, the only statewide requirement for high school graduation was two years of physical education. Students could enter college very easily but, lacking adequate literacy and numeracy, many enrolled in remedial college courses or soon dropped out.

There was a palpable sense that something needed to be done to improve the standards of education. The galvanizing event was the publication of *A Nation at Risk* in 1983. This was the earth-shattering report presented by the National Commission on Excellence in Education.

A Nation at Risk was a landmark of educational reform literature. Written in stirring language that the general public could understand, the report warned that the nation would suffer if education were not dramatically improved for all children. It also asserted that lax academic standards were correlated with lax behavioral standards and that neither should be ignored. This was a call to action. The commission recommended that all high school graduates study the new basics: four years of English and three years each of math, science, and social studies.

At the same time that the public expected progress toward higher standards, American education was plunged into divisive controversies about how schools should respond to the growing racial and ethnic diversity of pupils. In the late 1980s, multiculturalism became a hotly debated issue. Teachers and administrators agreed it was a good idea to add more materials about different cultures. The curriculum changed again!

Behind the uproar about multiculturalism came the self-esteem movement. The achievement gap between white students and students of color could be closed if low-performing students had higher self-esteem.

In the 1980s and 1990s, globalization was also transforming the American economy. The collapse of the Soviet Union and the end of the Cold War, coupled with the rapid development of new technologies, promoted change once again. New technology eliminated many unskilled jobs altogether and placed a premium on well-educated workers who understood math, science, and technology and were prepared both to exercise individual initiative and to work in teams.

Employers complained about the cost of teaching basic skills to entry-level workers and legislators worried about the cost and quality of education. International tests showed American high school students ranking below average in math and science.

Eager to improve the quality of education, state legislators and business leaders pressed for higher standards in the schools. Albert Shanker, president of the American Federation of Teachers, led this movement. He urged the creation of a national system of standards and assessments.

The 1990s saw the launch of federally approved grants to scholars and teachers for the development of national standards in seven school subjects (science, history, geography, the arts, civics, foreign languages, and English). The National Council of Teachers of Mathematics had already created its own standards.

These standards were supposed to describe what children should be expected to learn in different grades in every major academic subject. These standards were also intended to create a coherent framework of academic expectations that could be used by teachers, educators, textbook publishers, and standardized test developers.

President Clinton's first major educational legislation, called Goals 2000, was enacted in 1994. The program provided funds for states to develop standards and assessments. The first major standard for publication, in 1994, was for history. This was quickly followed by English standards.

The debate about reading reopened and it became phonics versus whole language once again. Whole language was a rebellion against drills, workbooks, textbooks, and other paraphernalia associated with phonics. Reformers said that if we surround children with a rich environment and provide lots of opportunities to read and write, children will learn to read without direct instruction about the sounds that letters represent. Whole-language learning involved student-centered activities, "authentic" reading experiences, integration of reading and writing, and freeing teachers from skill instruction.

However, in 1996, whole language received an unexpected setback. State-by-state reading scores revealed that those states using whole language were at the bottom of the list. By 1999, reformers concluded that both phonics and comprehension were necessary components of learning to read.

Throughout the curriculum wars of the 1990s, the message was clear: teachers must use their knowledge and experience to instruct their students, not stand aside and allow them to construct their own knowledge. Teachers must be teachers, not facilitators.

As we near the end of the first decade of the twenty-first century, the debates about standards and the concept of knowledge remain constantly under attack. What is clear today is that educators and the general public believe and emphasize that students can learn if the expectations for them are high enough and if they are taught in an orderly classroom environment. The public also wants students to learn good work habits and the value of effort. Parents, regardless of race, want the schools to focus on academic achievement and make sure students master the basics.

The history of education in America is the history of attempts to reform it. Yet, to the critics, change seemed impossible within the walls of urban public schools. However, there is a lesson to be learned from the river of ink that was spilled in the education disputes and reforms of the twentieth century. It is that anything in education that is labeled a movement should be carefully scrutinized and maybe even avoided like the plague. We need more attention to fundamental, time-tested truths. It is a fundamental truth that children need teachers who are willing to use different strategies depending on what works best for which child. It is another fundamental truth that adults must take responsibility for children and help them to become civic-minded adults.

Massive changes in curriculum and pedagogy should be based on solid research and careful field-tested demonstration before these changes are imposed on the school districts. Schools must be flexible enough to try new instructional methods and organizational patterns, and intelligent enough to gauge their results and success over time in accomplishing their primary mission: educating children.

As we take a walk though the history of educational reform in America, we note that Thomas Jefferson imagined an aristocracy of intellect, made up in part of "youths of genius" who would be raised by public education "from among the classes of the poor" (Kidder, 1989, p. 299).

Horace Mann, the great spokesman of the common school movement, imagined in the mid-nineteenth century a system of universal education for America which would make "the wheel of progress" roll "harmoniously and resistlessly onward" (p. 299).

John Dewey imagined schools that would provide for every child "an embryonic community life" and, for the nation, "the deepest and best guarantee of a larger society which is worthy, lovely, and harmonious" (p. 305).

W. E. B. DuBois imagined that education would someday help to bring about "the treatment of all men according to their individual desert and not according to their race" (p. 308).

James Bryant Conant, the president of Harvard and a leading voice for educational reform from around the end of World War II until the mid-1960s, imagined that public schools would answer the threat of Soviet Russian competition and "secure the foundations of our free society" (p. 309).

What great hopes Americans have placed in formal education. What a stirring faith in children and in the possibility and power of universal academic improvement.

For more than three hundred years public schools have helped to make us who we are as Americans. I do not see any more effective way to achieve a dynamic and successful future for our children than debating together and working together on how we educate our next generation.

2

The Change Process:
A Quiet Revolution

Everyone wants to change, but change demands desire and discipline before it becomes delightful. There is always the agony of choice before the promise of change.

—Larry Lea

American schools are in a mess. If you don't already know this, just take a look at the bleak statistics that have emerged over the past ten years. Kids simply aren't learning. They may be pulling down more As and Bs than ever before because of inflated grades, but they are not getting an education. They can't organize a paragraph (much less an essay), identify Winston Churchill (much less Charlemagne), understand Dickens (much less Shakespeare), understand main ideas in a test (much less infer meanings), separate major issues in a political campaign (much less handle their ambiguity), name the capital of Germany (much less find Iraq on a map), or calculate percentages (much less figure out the cost per item in the supermarket). Besides, SAT and ACT scores are falling, truancy and dropout rates are rising, and our unanswered cries for help are getting louder.

One of the most-touted reasons for our schools' poor report card is a lack of funds, but despite its role as a fall guy, the scarcity of money is not the chief reason. The real reason for failure in our schools lies not in absent dollars, but in our own willingness to sit around in despair. While we adults complain—and it's all of us (parents, teachers, administrators, and the whole disgruntled community)—children continue to be poorly educated. Thousands of kids out there can't read or write, or compute above an elementary school level, and worse yet, have not been taught to think at all.

We should stop laying the blame on money and start looking for solutions within the budgets we have. By we, I mean all of us, because what happens in our schools today determines what happens in our world tomorrow.

Change becomes possible when individuals with different roles interact around a shared concern for learning. Change may grow from seeds already planted in different schools and programs across the nation, fed by a constant flow of human energy interacting across all levels of school organization. Human energy is the key to school reform. Most of this energy for change comes from those who are closest to the ground, teachers and students in the classroom.

A school's successful change should be viewed over a long period of time, measured in terms of student achievement, professional growth and leadership, facilities development, ethical conduct, parental relationships, and school reputation. Change involves helping schools to redesign themselves in order to achieve their goals.

Can we get the degree of change and improvement we need in education by relying only on fixing the schools we now have? Do we need new schools that are fundamentally different? Will the public allow these new schools to emerge and create an environment in which they can succeed? I say both can be accomplished. We can change the schools we have and also create new ones. There is an urgent need to better understand, respect, and address the individual differences in students.

The change process has been underway in the educational system in America. The following is an example of how change brought local culture and academic success together.

Something special is happening in Russian Mission, Alaska. Just three years ago, one-third of the children ages twelve through sixteen were not attending school. Now every child of school age is in school.

Three years ago there was great concern about test scores because they were among the lowest in the district. Last year six seniors passed all three sections of the Alaska High School Graduation Qualifying Exam, and the other two passed writing. Russian Mission's ten third-graders achieved advanced or proficient scores on all sections of the benchmark test. Changes that are this broad-based are not merely the product of great teachers but also include family and community support.

Members of the school staff and community targeted the junior high because that was the age group that was dropping out of school. A curriculum was designed based on the subsistence activities of each season. Young people of that age have a lot of energy, do not do well in confined spaces, and are trying to define their places in the world. Traditionally these adolescents would have begun learning the roles of young men and women getting prepared by the community to take positions of responsibility.

The school sent these students to camp for two weeks in the fall. They caught fish, picked berries, learned about medicinal plants, cooked, and climbed mountains. While doing this they recorded their activities with digital cameras and laptop computers. When they came home they processed all the information and developed web pages to share their adventures with others. They became storytellers to the global community.

When in the classroom, much of their reading and writing focused on the wildlife in the area as well as local history. They studied their world. Then they went out, on a weekly basis, for experience-based learning with local experts. They went ice fishing and set rabbit and beaver snares and blackfish traps. They learned how to skin beavers and build snow shelters. And when they came home, they told their stories.

The activities set a pace for the students that carried over into the classroom. Kids who had never seen a beaver lodge snared and skinned their first beaver. The same kids raised their reading level by more than a year in just five months.

Junior high students are, by circumstance of their own developmental level, self-conscious and even self-centered. So why not make them and their world the things they read and write about? They are trying to find out who they are—show them. They want to know their place in the world—bring them into their world.

This is but one element of what is taking place at Russian Mission. The school has done nothing more than integrate into its program the skills necessary to sustain life in a subsistence setting. Isn't that the purpose of education, to acquire the skills one needs to lead a productive life in one's community? By doing this, the school has made a statement about the value of traditional skills and the value of culture. Students study their heritage and practice it, and it is working. It is gratifying to see young people excited about what they are doing and even more special to see them excited about who they are. Perhaps the community of Russian Mission, Alaska, has come to acknowledge the value of school because the school has come to acknowledge the value of the local heritage?

One cannot understand our complex society without understanding the history and culture of its ethnic and cultural components. We cannot understand American history, nor the social and political phenomena of the present, without understanding the African American, American Indian, Alaska Native, Latino, and Asian peoples' experiences as well as the varied groups who helped shape our institutions.

The dynamics of today's world require a new approach to learning. Rather than tinkering with the current educational practices, aiming at improving the situation, we should approach the current crisis of schooling from a completely different perspective. The need to learn and how to provide multicultural learning opportunities through a variety of flexible delivery mechanisms form the basis of this new perspective.

How can we teach teachers how to learn? We must embrace lifelong learning: learning to live. Today's world is rapidly changing, moving toward a more open and global society, bringing opportunities for economic growth, peace, human rights, and international partnership. We hear this all the time. But this change is also creating new sets of problems related to changing patterns of labor, multicultural societies, and environmental disruptions. Knowledge is dynamic: what is true today may have no value tomorrow. At the same time, access to information is perceived to be vital to economic development and power. We are responsible for the selection of relevant, useful, and accurate information. Knowing this, why do schools fail to provide the learning opportunities required in today's communities? Why don't schools require new ways to both access and look at the quality of education and learning? Why aren't schools creating learning environments?

The capability to cope with change requires the capacity to learn. The challenge lies in stimulating the learners' ability to build and enhance their own knowledge structures that are flexible and adaptable. In order to create effective learning opportunities I suggest that we use an integrated model of learning that involves classroom teaching as well as interaction with other learning channels such as family members, others in the community, social experiences, other learners, and a variety of media sources. Teachers should be encouraged to link up more actively with their communities. Take the opportunity to engage in learning whenever and wherever required.

All great teachers, from Socrates and Confucius to Dewey and Tyler, have become influential and inspirational to others, not because of their training or lack of training in materials and methods, but rather because of their human dimensions that give life to their meaningful messages. The best teachers are those who are able to translate their knowledge, wisdom, and experience into a form of communication that is compelling and interesting. Although teachers know that content is important, students could care less what they are teaching; what matters most to them is the style in which such knowledge and wisdom is imparted.

Teachers are often called upon to do so much more than impart knowledge. They influence children through the quality of their relationships and the power of their personalities.

However, teachers struggle with several obstacles: limitations of the school environment and the stress of interpersonal relationships with administration, colleagues, and difficult students. Teachers also struggle with esteem issues, as well as a sense of powerlessness and lack of teacher efficiency.

Let me give you some secrets to success: talk to your students; get to know them and their hopes, fears, and dreams; find gifts in each one; build on strengths; be interested and interesting; and take care of yourself.

All teachers have moments when they step back and say to themselves, "Wow! This is what teaching is all about. Something went right today. I wish I knew what it was!"

Classroom design can be a clue. Let your design include many forms, from letting students correct their own homework, to organizing their own games for recess, to attending their own teacher/parent conferences (presenting their own portfolio of work and explaining it), to teachers inviting students to challenge them.

Embrace the concepts that all children can learn and all children are valuable. I urge teachers to create a legal, safe, and passionate classroom, espousing personal mastery and team learning. Remember, we teach who we are.

What is the point of education? Is it to socialize young people so they can all fit into the fabric of society, to train a work force, or, best yet, to help young people learn how to create the lives they truly want to create? We must consider this question because there is no such thing as a regular child.

Teaching is an anomalous profession. Unlike doctors or lawyers, teachers do not share rules and obligations that they set for themselves. There are many communities that consider teachers servants and have not always treated them as well.

America has invested an enormous amount of faith in the idea of education, but not much in teachers. We must change this. A slow revolution in the reform movement must allow teachers to take charge of their practice and to shoulder more responsibility for hiring, mentoring, and promoting their peers. If you place teachers with different backgrounds and abilities in the same room and allow then to speak to each other as equal members you are empowering even the most timid and least skilled to survive.

The current portrait of teachers (most of them women) shows a struggle to take control of their practice in a system dominated by an administrative elite (mostly male). Better teachers will save the educational system. We must attract more talented recruits, help develop their skills, and institute better means of assessing teachers' performance. American schoolteachers are overwhelmingly female and white. Teachers of color are underrepresented in the teaching force. We must make changes.

Teachers play a major role in the reform process. Before we can embrace any changes we need to ask ourselves, how do you know a good teacher if you see one? To be a good teacher is to hold one of the most difficult and at the same time most satisfying jobs imaginable.

I believe a good teacher is excited about learning and helping students learn; truly cares about the kids; reaches out to them; does not see them as the enemy or assume a confrontational stance with them; and creates a we/we environment, not a we/they environment. A good teacher is alert to teachable moments and is flexible enough to grab these golden opportunities. A good teacher does not fall apart in face of such trivia as students occasionally being late to class, missing a class, or not having a pass, but keeps his or her eye on the target of helping students to learn and grow, to work hard, to think, and to question.

There is more. A good teacher is knowledgeable about the subject matter, in perspective. Indeed, a good teacher knows that the subject matter is rarely as important to students as other matters in their lives (coping with growing up, developing their own values, relating to peers and adults, and checking out the world around them).

Is all this possible? Yes, but it is not easy. It takes hard work and energy to develop and maintain relationships with young people. It is worthwhile and satisfying. The energy it takes causes a relaxed tiredness at day's end, not the angry, exhausted tiredness many teachers frequently feel. It is rewarding. It is necessary if our goal is to help students become enlightened, knowledgeable, questioning, self-directed adults.

How do students know a good teacher when they see one? They do not have the same perceptions. Different teacher characteristics are important for different students. Yet there are some common threads. Listen to what the students have to say:

There are certain teachers I have to thank. They give me knowledge and skills, which allow me to live. Others placed the blame on me, saying I can't learn anything. I saw their bad attitudes.

- As a teacher you acted human and showed compassion.
- Now I see why I need to learn on my own, no teacher threats. You give a damn.
- I want a teacher who won't give up on me.
- I like a teacher who will pressure me so I push myself harder.

So how can we get teachers like the ones the kids want and need? Reform must include teaching the teachers.

Teacher training is a major problem. Most people go through teacher training programs and find out much of it is not very helpful. This could be the subject of a whole book in itself. It will be discussed only briefly here.

Teacher training can be described as society's missed opportunity. "Teachers and teacher educators do not know enough about subject matter, they don't know enough about how to teach, and they don't know enough about how to understand and influence the conditions around them.

Above all, teacher education, from initial preparation to end of career, is not geared towards continuing learning" (Fullan, 2003, p. 108).

Teachers often operate in isolation; they mostly have no opportunity to reflect on their own practice or to exchange experiences and ideas with colleagues due to high work pressure and/or the necessity of having more than one full-time job. At the same time, those teachers who are enthusiastic, capable, and highly motivated are frustrated with their contribution to change, and quite often a supporting and understanding environment seems to be lacking.

Triggering teachers to initiate change processes does not involve the imposition of measures by school management but rather should be the result of self-motivated processes of learning by the teachers.

Throughout the years I have identified four aspects of the teacher as learner that are critical in the improvement of classroom practice: development of the instructional repertoire in teachers; development of reflective practice, which facilitates clarity, meaning, and coherence; stimulation of research activities to develop an attitude of investigation and exploration; and promotion of collaboration with colleagues, which enables teachers to exchange experiences and receive and give ideas, feedback, and assistance.

Classrooms and schools centered on learning and learners are intellectually rigorous places, exciting, and humane. They are concerned with honoring individuality, developing potential, and arming students with the ability to think freely and independently.

Good schools allow teachers to flourish; reduce bureaucratic demands, favoring competence over procedure; nurture and reward professional development; support curricula and assessments that are relevant and challenging; and stimulate inside-out change. We must seek opportunities that will allow teachers to become learners, challenging them in a process of professional development in order to develop those skills and practices that are most constructive in the learning communities they are a part of. This cannot be done in isolation but in collaboration and partnership between teacher educators, teachers, and specialists, as well as students and their parents.

There needs to be a perceptual change among teachers to see themselves as learners as well as facilitators of the learning process.

Right now there appears to be a lack of congruence between teacher training and the experience teachers find in the classrooms. They need to understand the difference between the training program and reality. If teacher training included self-awareness experiences, it might provide prospective teachers with some psychological tools necessary to deal with the system. Then they would be less likely to be taken in or dragged down by it. Instead, the training most teachers receive includes very little about child or adolescent behavior, let alone about teacher behavior in general. It seldom touches on the need to know oneself well if one is to work effectively and nonconfrontationally with students.

Part of this is because most teacher training programs are part of the same system as the schools. The training colleges have a big stake in things as they are. A kind of old-boy network develops between teacher training colleges and the schools. Prospective teachers are not encouraged to challenge the schools' premises or the we/they atmosphere that is the norm. The net result is that most people complete teacher training with a minimum knowledge about themselves and how to realistically cope with schools. They have not learned or may never learn how to effectively challenge faulty premises about how learning takes place.

Once on the job, neophyte teachers find it easier and safer to follow the formal and informal rules of the system. They fall into the clutches of experienced teachers, who often are very cynical about kids and learning new methods about dealing with them. "This is the way kids are and this is the way the system operates and don't buck it; don't come up with all this newfangled stuff," is a common line new teachers hear. These new teachers have to be unusually tough, secure, and aware to be able to withstand that. Often new teachers are pulled down to the level of the older teachers because they cave in, hoping to gain some status and favor, much in the same way oppressed people sometimes deal with their oppressors. And then the older teachers' behavior becomes a habit with the newer teachers until they, too, become cynical older teachers.

What can teachers do? Change! They can change their teaching methods to encourage students to become excited about learning instead of promoting boredom. Teachers can move away from busywork assignments that turn students off and toward more creative, long-range project–style assignments.

Teachers who give nightly homework assignments do not call this busywork. They are trying to force students to study and learn, but that is not the result for most kids. Those students who usually do the assignments do so not because they think they learn from them but because it is the only way to get a good grade. Students who refuse to do the assignments are rebelling. For these kids, the lure of the grade is not great enough to overcome their rebellion.

Society has missed an opportunity. It is apparent that teacher reform has gone astray. Teacher preparation programs need substantial improvement. It appears too many teachers are drawn from the bottom of their high school and college classes; teacher preparation curriculum is heavy on methods and light on subject matter; the pay is too low and teachers have little influence over critical professional decisions (i.e., textbook/materials selection); and at least half of the newly employed teachers of core subjects are "not highly qualified."

To solve these problems I would recommend: would-be teachers should be required to demonstrate an aptitude for teaching and prove competence in an academic discipline; teacher salaries should be increased (to be both market sensitive and performance-based); career ladders should be established for teachers so they can gain in status and pay; there should be incentives to attract outstanding students to teaching; and master teachers should be allowed to design teacher preparation programs and supervise novice instructors.

Despite all our recommendations, the same problems remain with us: low academic standards for new teachers; "alternative routes" into teaching that are still filled with requirements; far too many waivers in math, science, and special education for people who lack any certification or other qualifications; and the failure of most states to tie their standards for teachers to those for students.

These problems are now widely recognized. We're more mindful of shortages of competent instructors in key fields, we're more sensitive to problems like the out-of-field teaching personnel, and we're more keenly aware of how important teachers are to children's education, particularly for the most sorely disadvantaged youngsters.

The solutions urged earlier have not been embraced. Unions chew away at career ladders until they collapse; performance-based pay seems to be linked to supervisor or peer judgments, not to student achievement; and alternative certification programs have slid back into the clutches of the colleges of education.

What went wrong? To make the changes suggested would mean altering deeply entrenched practices and challenging the sturdiest bastions of the education establishment (teacher unions, colleges of education, and state education bureaucracies). It would mean training people differently, licensing them differently, paying them differently (and differentially), and judging them differently. This has not happened. The forces arrayed on behalf of such changes were not half as strong as those massed to repel reform.

Maybe we should change our focus from teachers as instruments of school improvement to teachers as *shapers* of school improvement, from teachers as staff in an educational system run by others to teachers as key decision makers about the purpose and operation of the system itself. We should shift power from those who would improve the schools from the outside to educators themselves.

How do we go forward? First, we must agree to focus on student achievement. Student learning must be our primary focus and chief tracking system. Second, we should be open-minded and experimental. Nobody should have the power to veto a promising approach that benefits students on the grounds that it doesn't appeal to adults who work in the schools. Third, place teachers in charge of their schools by letting them have a voice in who is qualified to teach. Fourth, when it comes to teacher preparation, let some be trained by teacher colleges, but let others enter the classroom through alternate routes and programs.

The list could be extended, but the point is clear: too many of today's educational reform debates are conducted as if they were winner-take-all contests that must leave a single reform strategy standing. So let's try multiple approaches. Let's declare a truce in the teacher wars and try to figure out what works best.

I ask you to take a brief look at an alternate certification plan that helped New Jersey solve its teacher problems. New Jersey's Board of Education realized that their schools varied widely in enrollment, funding, location, methodology, and quality, yet the most fundamental implement of the state's educational policy is the teacher. The problem in New Jersey and most other states is teacher quantity. Shortages are particularly acute in certain subject areas (math, science, and special education). Their second issue, as in many states, is teacher quality. In most states, the criteria by which a teacher may be deemed qualified include a college degree; full certification or licensure, with no waivers of certification; and demonstration of subject matter competence. The key to improving teacher quality may not lie in credentialing measures, but in attracting more qualified individuals to the field in the first place.

The New Jersey Department of Education chose an alternative certification plan as a means of addressing the growing teacher quality and teacher quantity problems. The New Jersey public schools removed the formal certification requirements and adopted a protocol by which one could be deemed a qualified teacher without official licensure. The guidelines were a college degree in the teaching-area subject, an extensive criminal background check, a passing score on subject-knowledge test, participation in an eight-month mentoring program with a veteran teacher, and completion of an accelerated two-hundred-hour teacher training course with emphasis on pedagogy, psychology, and curriculum development.

New Jersey believes that the most important goal of licensure reform is to improve the quality of teachers and thereby improve the quality of schools; traditional certification requirements are one of the most onerous barriers preventing highly qualified candidates from exploring teaching careers. The New Jersey plan was successful in attracting applicants with high verbal ability and subject-matter knowledge, two of the teacher traits most closely linked to student performance.

Another approach, currently favored in New York state, emphasizes improving teacher training programs and tightening the requirements for entering teaching. Two problems face this approach, however. There is little evidence that differences in teacher performance are related to teacher training, and regulatory approaches tend to restrict entry into teaching, which could be a serious problem in areas where there are shortages already.

The state of New York has begun a sweeping reform of elementary, middle, and secondary education in an effort to improve school quality. The efforts have been focused both on raising all achievement and on improving the outcomes for less advantaged students. Recognizing that high-quality teachers are the key to effective schools, New York has concentrated its efforts on dramatic reforms in the way it recruits, prepares, certifies, and continues to educate teachers. The basic issue in recruitment is whether to loosen or tighten entry requirements.

The specifics of the New York state blueprint for teacher reform reveal a program that combines more stringent demands on current and future teachers and schools of education with additional support for teacher recruitment and training plus financial incentives for college students to select teaching as a career, particularly teaching in low-income and minority neighborhoods. New York feels that more stringent certification requirements (elimination of temporary and emergency certification), rigorous exams, and a focused continuing education program appear to ensure a dramatic improvement in teacher quality and in the academics in the schools.

What do we really know about teacher quality? Students and parents act to ensure placement in classes with specific teachers. Administration looks at the contribution of teachers to differences in student outcomes. We also know that teachers improve markedly in the first and second years on the job, but there are no significant gains or losses in teacher effectiveness from additional experience. The comparison of teacher effect and family differences provides another perspective. Families appear to exert a much more important effect than schools.

In order to promote change, we must ask ourselves even more questions. Why does teacher effectiveness vary greatly within one school building? Is the hiring process inadequate? Do tenure procedures fail to identify low-performing teachers? Is there a great deal of variation in effort or skill? Why doesn't the acquisition of a master's degree lead to systematic improvement in the quality of instruction?

The answers to these questions relate directly to the crafting of reforms of school policy relating to teachers. The research does not provide direct answers for all questions, but three patterns are emerging: the distinction between more and less effective teachers cannot be made simply on the basis of visible characteristics such as degree, experience, certification, test scores, or college attended; the weak link between teacher quality and the possession of a master's degree indicates that the current school structure does not induce graduate schools of education to offer programs that raise teacher effectiveness; and following the first two years of teaching, the additional return on experience is quite small.

It seems to me that if everyone is concerned about student performance then we should gear change in policy to student performance. The problem with the current organization of schools is that nobody's job or career is closely related to student performance. This must change. Mentoring and support, tenure review, and the management of experienced teachers leave tremendous room for improvement. Principals and superintendents cannot be expected to work magic, particularly in economically disadvantaged communities. But the fact remains that an accurate set of performance measures for teachers and schools should be an integral piece of the education reform process.

The new trend is to focus on incentives and school leadership. Give those who manage schools the appropriate incentives to succeed and let them have the flexibility to provide teachers with similar motivation. This would lead teachers to seek the best possible training and professional development. We must recognize and admit that we have problems. We never seem to learn much from the policies we put into place. In fact, schools frequently make policy decisions in ways that defy ever learning about their effects.

I mentioned professional development as a necessary component of teacher quality. Let's explore this concept further.

Almost every approach to school reform requires teachers to refocus their roles, responsibilities, and opportunities and, as a result, to acquire new knowledge and skills. Teaching to high standards, however, requires many educators to teach in ways they have never taught before. There is a dramatic difference between the way teachers learned during their apprenticeship as students or novice teachers in traditional classrooms and effective innovations of today. Like students, teachers must be actively involved in learning and must have opportunities to discuss, reflect upon, try out, and hone better instructional approaches. If teacher learning takes place within a professional community that is nurtured and developed from both inside and outside the school, significant and lasting school change may follow. Engaging in an array of learning experiences with school colleagues builds community and reduces isolation. Teachers need professional development that extends beyond the one-shot workshop; they need opportunities to learn how to question, analyze, and change instruction to teach challenging content.

High-quality professional development often supports teachers in new and expanded roles as teacher leaders, peer advisors, and teacher researchers. Most importantly teachers need to create a culture of continuous professional development where learning together becomes expected behavior. In addition, teachers also need to make use of the opportunities available for teacher learning outside of school (collaborations with formal and informal networks and partnerships with community groups).

New thinking about professional development places teachers' learning opportunities at the center of school restructuring. But if professional development is integral to school life and change, then professional learning must also apply to other educators: counselors, aides, and especially principals. Like teachers, principals need to engage in activities that examine teaching, shared decision making, and student achievement and learning.

In conclusion, professional development is most effective when it is accessible to all educators and is part of a systemwide effort to improve teacher recruitment, selection, preparation, licensing and certification, and ongoing development and support. Strong professional development programs require partnerships among schools, higher educational institutions, and other entities to promote learning opportunities for all involved.

Overall professional development focuses on teachers as central to student learning, yet includes the entire school community; establishes improvement; respects and nurtures; reflects the best available research; enables teachers to develop further expertise in subject content, strategies, and use of technology; is planned collaboratively; requires time; and is evaluated on the basis of its effects on teachers' instruction and student achievement and uses this assessment to guide subsequent professional development efforts.

As efforts to increase standards of teaching and learning take hold, their success hinges on the extent to which teachers change their roles, responsibilities, and practices to be more effective. In addition, their success depends on the support given as teachers strive to meet the challenges of guiding all students to reach high standards.

Teachers must become change agents and teacher education programs must be prepared to assist teachers in developing the tools that will prepare them to engage in productive change.

Most teachers begin their careers with a sense that their work is socially meaningful and will yield great personal satisfaction. This sense dissipates, and they become disheartened as the inevitable difficulties of teaching interact with personal issues and vulnerabilities as well as social pressure and values. All this causes a sense of frustration and reassessment of the job and the investment one wants to make in it. Teachers close to the needs of children and youth advocate for change and go on to develop better strategies for reaching their goals. Those skilled in change appreciate its volatile character, and they explicitly seek means for coping with and influencing change toward some desired ends.

I see four core capacities for teachers which result in building change. Personal vision building means examining and reexamining why we came into teaching. Inquiry is the engine of vitality and self-renewal necessary for forming and reforming personal purpose, as teachers as change agents are lifelong learners. Mastery involves a new mindset, which leads to new ideas and where they fit in. Mastery combines specific innovations and personal habits. Collaboration is one of the core requisites of society and evolves to getting the right things done.

But we are facing a huge dilemma. On one hand, schools are expected to engage in continuous renewal, and change expectations are constantly swirling around them. On the other hand, the way teachers are trained, the way schools are organized, the way the educational hierarchy operates, and the way political decisionmakers treat educators result in a system that is more likely to retain the status quo. To break the impasse, we need a new conception of teacher professionalism that integrates change.

Despite the rhetoric about teacher education today, there does not seem to be a real belief that investing in teacher education will yield results. Currently, teacher education, from initial preparation throughout the career, is not geared toward continuous learning. Teacher education institutions themselves must take responsibility for their current reputation as laggards rather than leaders of educational reform. Teacher educators, like other would-be change agents, must take some initiative themselves.

We must start by redesigning the teacher preparation program. I propose that every teacher should be knowledgeable about, committed to, and skilled in working with *all* students by respecting diversity; being active learners; developing knowledge of curricula, instruction, and evaluation; initiating, valuing, and practicing collaboration; being aware of the ethical and legal responsibilities of teaching as a profession; and developing a personal philosophy of teaching.

To summarize, facilities of education must redesign their programs to focus directly on developing the beginner's knowledge base for effective teaching and the knowledge base for changing the conditions that affect teaching. These teachers' colleges must focus on the fact that teachers of the future must be equally at home in the classroom and in working with others to bring about continuous improvements. To restructure is not to reculture.

The teacher of the future must actively improve the conditions for learning in his or her immediate environment. Teachers will never improve learning in the classroom unless they also help improve conditions that surround the classroom. To do this teachers should listen to their inner voices, practice reflection in action, develop a risk-taking mentality, commit to working with colleagues, redefine their roles to extend beyond the classroom, balance work and life, and commit to lifelong learning.

Teacher professionalism is at a threshold. Change is implicit in what good teaching and effective change are about. Are they society's great untapped resources for radical and continuous improvement? Maybe we need to go public with a new rationale for why teacher and teacher development are fundamental to the future of society.

Change is a constant for schools. Like earlier drives for reform, the current one aims to improve students' academic achievement. The focus is on rethinking and restructuring schools to serve all students well. Curriculum and instruction are being modified in several schools to engage all students and to articulate programs across grade levels. Central to any reform is the involvement of staff members in decision making. Traditional hierarchical structures must give way to more collaborative structures. This entails changing the way administrators, students, teachers, and parents relate to each other. The goal is to reconceptualize and renew the school's total operation from within, as that reform is tailored to local conditions and teachers are committed to what they have helped to craft.

Change within a school usually requires that the whole staff take stock of their practices and devise new directions. This may mean modifying traditional beliefs and practices to respond more accurately to students' learning needs. One useful mechanism for change is inquiry groups, in which teachers raise questions, gather and analyze data, and plan responses.

Current views of change within schools also emphasize strengthening and transforming school relationships with parents and the community to make them more collaborative. Regardless of income or level of education, parents can support children's education, for example, by reading with them and talking to them. Even if the parents' own level of literacy is low, they can offer support when they encourage an inquiry approach to learning in the home. Schools need to develop partnerships with parents that allow them to identify and validate such parental contributions to the shared task of educating students. A dinner event can go a long way in strengthening relationships among families, school staff, businesses, and the community.

Reforming schools to serve all students takes time. Change has been characterized as a process that is incremental, chaotic, and ongoing. None of the elements that contribute to effective change is easily or quickly achieved. Building a collaborative, professional community with strong, committed leadership; using teacher inquiry and reflection as vehicles for improving instruction and professional development; and inventing and preserving connections among the school, the parents, and the community—all of these must be seen as long-term, challenging processes.

It has been said many times that schools need to learn how to provide ongoing successful education for all students, education that helps them locate who they are and how they can make a contribution to the world; that stretches them to achieve high standards, yet affirms their basic humanity and right to pursue what matters most to them.

We need both the inner and outer views to gain understanding. Living and learning are inseparable. Students participate in the continual flow of experiences. Through the ability to reflect, these experiences become knowledge. This process begins with the first breath of life and continues through the threshold of death.

Schools are merely a way of forming and organizing the learning experiences that society believes are necessary for children. As schools have grown and developed over the years, they have become more important as organizations, and sometimes the "living and learning" aspects have receded in favor of "expectations and requirements," whether imposed by legislators, parents, or textbook publishers. From time to time, courageous advocates for change have stepped forth to redress the balance. These change advocates have always tried to refocus our attention on the needs of the child.

Prior reform and change efforts have not been buttressed by the ongoing professional development needed to prepare teachers to teach in the complex ways that learner-centered practice demands. Reforms have not been accompanied by policies that reinforce the pursuit of challenging forms of learning through associated changes in curriculum, resources, funding, teaching policies, and school organization. Finally, a public understanding of educational ideas and possibilities has not supported most reforms.

New models of reform must seek to develop communities of learning grounded in communities of democratic discourse. Only in this way can communities come to want for all their children what they want for their most advantaged, an education for empowerment and an education for freedom.

People don't fear change unless they're kept in the dark. Change is disturbing when it is done *to* us, exhilarating when it is done *by* us. Change requires the perception that there is crisis. Structure must change before culture can change. School reform is not partly politics, it is all politics.

3

Comprehensive School Reform

It is better to debate a question without settling it, than to settle a question without debating it.

—Joseph Joubert

Educating the next generation of Americans, the young people whose contributions and problems will shape the very future of our country, is the most important job anyone in a democracy can accomplish.

We need educators who see their jobs as worthwhile. We do not need people who have swallowed the argument that low-income children and African American, Latino, and American Indian children cannot achieve at high levels because poverty and discrimination create too many hurdles to learning.

When people tell us that it is unfair to expect the poorest children to reach high standards, we need to reply, "Unfair to whom? Surely in this era when anything less than a quality education sentences a young person to a life on the margins, you're not suggesting that aiming high is unfair to the children?"

As a nation, we've made a policy decision to no longer tolerate widespread failure in schools serving low-income children and children of color. We have decided all children should be taught to high standards, no matter what neighborhoods they live in or how poor their families are. We must continue our drive to reach this goal.

There have always been educators who have beaten the odds and achieved high levels of success with kids who have been written off by other teachers and administrators. Such educators have been shaping a new vision of what is possible. We must seek out these educators and use their successes in our educational reform motives. We must develop a hunger for information about what successful schools have done. We need concrete strategies and ways to improve and move schools forward. We must establish clear goals with high expectations and ongoing assessments. Each classroom needs a strong teacher who knows the subject content and knows how to teach it. A rigorous curriculum is part of the package, as well as giving extra help and extra time to students who are behind. This is a must and should be part of every school classroom and program. I firmly believe that if you teach low-income students and children of color at higher levels, they will achieve at higher levels. If you expect great things from children, they will produce great things.

That being said, now ask yourselves, "Can it be done? Can our current schools help *all* children learn to high levels, even children of color? Is it even possible for schools to help children who face the substantial obstacles of poverty and discrimination to learn how to read, write, compute, and generally become educated citizens?"

I have seen glimmers of hope in a fifth-grade classroom where American Indian boys and girls from the Little Earth projects met state math standards at higher rates than at any other school in the Twin Cities area. I have also seen hope in the extraordinary kindergarten class of Judy S., who could boast without fear of contradiction that, in thirty-plus years of teaching, she had taught just about every one of her students how to read.

However, I have never seen a whole school where the average child of color or child of poverty could walk in from the neighborhood and be pretty sure he or she would learn to read, do math, write, and otherwise succeed academically.

Instead I have seen suburban schools where middle-class and wealthy white children, particularly girls, seem to do well, but where the poor or students of color (African Americans, Latinos, American Indians), especially boys, do terribly.

I have also seen schools where most of the students are white and middle class or upper-middle class. These schools have high test scores and high SAT or ACT scores and have boasted that 95 percent to 100 percent of the students were accepted at a college.

I have seen what I call crummy poor-kid schools, inadequate schools that too many low-income students attend. I had the same edgy feeling I've felt in jails, as if something terrible could happen at any time. I encountered dull classrooms filled with worksheets and entertainment movies on televisions. I talked to teachers in these schools who told me, "These kids aren't like *your* kids," meaning that most of the students couldn't be expected to learn as much as white, middle-class children of college graduates. These teachers would also add that telling these kids to go to college would be a huge waste of time.

Instead of dedicating themselves to making sure all children learned to high standards, it seemed that the schools I visited simply sorted their students into different categories. The "high" students were offered what passed for a real education, although there was reliance on parents to provide a lot of the teaching. The "middle" kids were given some aspects of real teaching, and the "low" kids were babysat until they were old enough to drop out. In poor-kid schools, just about all students were considered "low." A lucky few were skimmed off into magnet schools, charter schools, or other special programs.

What we need are schools that are not just good schools for low-income children and children of color, but that are good for every child. These schools should be managed by dedicated, energetic, skilled professionals, who talk about the needs of children and who care very deeply about whether all their students have access to the kinds of knowledge and opportunities that most middle-class white children take for granted.

Some schools across the nation are improving, but we have a long way to go. Reform must continue. We have the important work of educating all our children within our grasp.

One approach to solving the problem of educating all our children fully falls under the realm of an improvement program known as "whole school" or Comprehensive School Reform (CSR). The CSR program is an important opportunity to improve entire schools and raise student achievement using scientifically based research and effective practices. Schools are given the opportunity to adopt comprehensive improvements with a track record of success.

The latter half of the twentieth century was marked by recurring efforts at school reform and improvement in the United States. Yet this cycle of reform, like a pendulum's swing, has continued to move from one fad to another with little evidence of national progress. As each new reform is widely disseminated and implemented, the research follow closely behind, sometimes weighing in on the issue only after schools have moved on to the next apparent innovation. Recent national reform and policy movements, though, may halt this frustrating cycle.

In addition to the focus on research-based solutions for school improvement, current CSR initiatives help reconcile the two most important educational reform movements in the United States. Since the 1980s, competing and often contradictory reforms have combined top-down, centralized efforts to improve schools and teaching with efforts at decentralization and school-based management. The general spirit of today's reform efforts continues to articulate top-down standards, which dictate much of the change in the content of schooling, but fundamentally leave the process of school change up to the discretion of local educators. The problem is that the complex educational changes demanded by current standards-based reform initiatives, combined with an increasingly heterogeneous student population largely composed of students whom schools have traditionally failed, have pushed the technology of schooling toward unprecedented levels of complexity.

In many ways, expecting local educators to reinvent the process of educational reform school by school is both unrealistic and unfair. Every child has the capacity to succeed in school and in life. Yet far too many children fail to meet their potential. Many students, especially those from poor families and families of color, are placed at risk by school practices that sort some students into high-quality programs and other students into low-quality education. I firmly believe that schools must replace the "sorting paradigm" with a reform model that sets high expectations for all students and ensures that all students receive a rich and demanding curriculum with appropriate assistance and support.

Furthermore, comprehensive reform must transform the schools to ensure the success of all students at key development points, building on students' personal and cultural assets and scaling up effective programs conducted through research and development: programs in the areas of early and elementary studies; middle and high school studies; school, family, and community partnerships; and systemic supports for school reform.

The CSR program began in 1998 and was authorized as Title I, part F of the Elementary and Secondary Education Act, which was signed into law on January 8, 2002. It is an important component of the No Child Left Behind (NCLB) Act. CSR is helping to raise student achievement by assisting public schools across the country in implementing effective, comprehensive school reforms. The program builds on and leverages ongoing state and local efforts to connect higher standards and school improvement. CSR also helps to expand the quality and quantity of schoolwide reform efforts that enable all children, particularly low-achieving children, to meet challenging academic standards. Hundreds of schools in all fifty states, the District of Columbia, Puerto Rico, and schools funded by the Bureau of Indian Affairs (BIA) have received grants as part of the original program.

The CSR program is designed to foster coherent, schoolwide improvements that cover virtually all aspects of a school's operations rather than piecemeal, fragmented approaches to reform. A key feature of the program is that it provides incentives for schools to develop comprehensive reform programs based on scientifically accepted research and effective practices. The reforms must help all children to meet challenging state academic content and achievement standards. Whether they use a nationally available approach or develop their own programs locally, these schools must coherently integrate the eleven components of a CSR program.

Schools are required to implement a CSR program that employs proven methods and strategies based on scientifically-based research; integrates a comprehensive design with aligned components; provides ongoing, high-quality professional development for teachers and staff; includes measurable goals and benchmarks for student achievement; is supported within the school by teachers, administrators, and staff; provides support for teachers, administrators, and staff; provides for meaningful parent and community involvement in planning, implementing, and evaluating school improvement activities; uses high-quality external technological support and assistance from an external partner with experience and expertise in schoolwide reform and improvement; plans for evaluation of strategies for the implementation of school reforms and for student results achieved annually; identifies resources to support and sustain the school's comprehensive reform efforts; and has been found to significantly improve the academic achievement of students or demonstrates strong evidence that it will improve the academic achievement of students.

CSR programs are not separate projects that are added on to existing programs. The entire educational operation must be improved through curriculum changes, sustained professional development, and enhanced involvement by parents, based on a careful identification of local needs.

Externally developed reform designs are consistent in that they provide a model for whole school change and help schools address many issues. At the same time, though, the externally developed designs are remarkably diverse in their analysis of the specific problems in U.S. education, the solutions that they propose, and the processes they propose for achieving those solutions. For example, the Comer School Development Program builds largely around Dr. James Comer's work in community psychiatry, focusing its energy on reforming or re-creating schools that address a wide range of students' health, social, emotional, and academic challenges (Comer, 1988). By contrast, the Core Knowledge reform (Hersch, 1995, 1996) derives from the developer's experiences as a professor of English and education, and focuses almost entirely on the establishment of a "common core" of knowledge for all children within various subject areas, including literature, history, science, mathematics, and the arts. The Coalition of Essential Schools comprehensive reform model attempts to create more educationally rich and supportive learning environments through a common adherence to nine broadly philosophical principles (Sizer, 1992), whereas Success for All (Slavin and Madden, 2001) provides a specific K–6 reading curriculum, professional development sequence, and other school-wide components.

Comprehensive school reform is meant to be undertaken by individual schools as well as large districts. The following is an example of a consolidated improvement plan that was the focus of a CSR program for a small, inner-city, low-income, American Indian charter school in Minneapolis, Minnesota.

The plan began with a detailed needs assessment that the school improvement team (select teachers and parents, consultants, principal, and board chairman) outlined. This included demographic data, achievement data, process data (showing current improvement in the areas of curriculum, instruction, textbook purchases, and instructional improvement, showing curriculum mapping), and performance data (including factors that impact student achievement such as truancy, educational neglect, foster care, homelessness, substance abuse, and health issues like dental care, vision, auditory issues, obesity, onset of diabetes, asthma, and mental health issues).

After reviewing the needs assessment, the team then addressed the planning requirements of a Comprehensive School Reform program. The team selected three promising vendor models from the Northeast Regional Education Laboratory website to evaluate. The team then reviewed three K–12 programs (More Effective Schools, Accelerated Schools, and Urban Learning Centers) to determine if the programs selected met the school's requirements as stated in the needs assessment. After reviewing the programs and realizing the challenge of documenting effectiveness of strategies, the team decided to develop its own plan.

Direct Instruction is on the federally approved list of acceptable models. AIMSweb Curriculum Based Measurement (CBM) Tools met scientific standards for use in frequent progress monitoring by the National Center on Student Progress Monitoring, funded by the U.S. Department of Education. The requirement for using external resources was fulfilled. All have been documented as research-based and effective. In addition, aligning curriculum, instruction, and assessments with state standards was completed. A table was then designed elaborating on strategies, theory, and research.

In order to move forward, each teacher was given a new laptop. Technology was to be used to track student performance at the formative level to monitor progress. Student fluency and math basic calculation expectations at various grade levels are carefully tracked. Classroom goals aligned to school goals are also monitored. Meeting the academic requirements of special education and mobile students will be accomplished in part by targeting specific skills and knowledge. An after-school study hall will give additional help in classroom needs. A key piece of this effort is that all teachers will know precisely what the target performance levels are.

Professional development at the school is aligned to inform, reinforce, and support all of the above (curriculum mapping, AIMSweb training, Direct Instruction, goal setting, etc.). Training will be repeated for new faculty in ensuing years. The entire faculty supported the reform effort.

The school also realized how critical parent and community involvement would be in securing a successful reform plan. A parent advisory advocacy committee was organized and provided direct input on such issues as curriculum, student conduct, parent support, student achievement, and so on. The committee will better facilitate support for education and communication to the community through personal contacts, meetings, and newsletters.

Finally, external technical assistance was sought. A reading consultant and an educational consultant were hired to provide additional services. The primary purpose was to help put structures in place, implement the reform plan, and provide ongoing mentoring and embedded staff development for an action plan in order to build capacity for the staff to continue the process.

To complete the plan, resources were explored and implemented. This included an IT consultant to provide technical assistance; a school social worker to provide assistance with student, home, and family issues; the University of Minnesota to provide student tutors; and Americorps members.

Evaluation of the reform plan will list the school's indicators of success. Data will be used on an ongoing basis to measure teacher effectiveness through student achievement. Results will be available for review. Student achievement as measured on formative assessments will be aggregated and disaggregated by classroom and building levels to determine effectiveness of instruction with individual students, groups of students, classrooms, and buildings. Staff is aware that adjustments in instruction can be made to improve achievement levels as the site moves toward its goals.

The staff firmly believed that with this CSR plan in place all students will reach high standards, attain their maximum potential, and attain proficiency or better in core subjects.

As we look more closely at CSR, several things continue to stand out. In today's educational crisis, many people are coming to realize that there is far more to a school reform plan than imparting knowledge and skills and administering tests. Schools are also communities and must address the many unseen dimensions of each student and family.

Wider social, political, economic, and intellectual movements have always determined the character of educational thought and practice in the United States. The Russian launching of *Sputnik* in 1957 influenced and dramatically changed school practice in the nation. In the 1980s and 1990s, the challenge to U.S. business and technology enterprises by foreign markets influenced the character of educational thought. The lightning rod this time was not a foreign country's satellite, but the National Commission on Excellence in Education report *A Nation at Risk* (1983). This report placed the major part of the responsibility for the invasion on technology (e.g., Sony televisions) and automobiles (e.g., Hyundai) on the American educational system. The report stated, "If only to keep and improve on the slim competitive edge we still retain in world markets, we must rededicate ourselves to the reform of the educational system for the benefit of all" (p. 7). The reform discourse then became the character of educational thought and practice. Federal, state, and local political leaders and officials took control of this discourse. They directed it toward a return to the basics. "Back to the basics," "excellence and accountability," and the "new basics" became educational reform slogans. The policymakers demanded that we be tough on schools and on teachers and students. They would win elections based on this, so it was believed.

Reform leaders must be willing to become entrepreneurs and be the opposite of a bureaucrat. You can't follow the rules blindly; you keep an eye focused on your main goal, which is to help students succeed. Our comprehensive reform movement must change the way schools are managed. We need to operate under this rule, "That it is easier to ask forgiveness for ones actions after taking action than to ask permission beforehand. Be accountable for results." It is entirely within the realm of possibility to reform our schools.

Our schools continue to fail; everyone knows it. School board meetings have become battlefields as angry parents are on the attack. State legislatures have admitted it, and the media expounds it.

When reform comes into play, it appears educators tend to look at three common theories about this school failure. First, teachers aren't any good, and they are the source of the failure. Second, the students, especially inner-city students of color, simply aren't able or willing to learn. Third, we have to spend more money on our schools to improve them.

I submit that all three are wrong. Consider this: when a business is failing, the owners don't blame the customers, the front-line employees, or the budget—they go after the management and shake them up. There is nothing wrong with the students or the teachers, and many school systems have enough money to do the job. Could it be the management that needs to be changed? Good management both attracts dedicated teachers and creates the environment in which all teachers do their best every day. Comprehensive reform must include school leaders and management teams.

I would like to offer reformers seven keys to success. Every principal is an entrepreneur, one who fights for the teachers and students every day, hangs out there taking chances, and gets no thanks for his or her accomplishments; control your budget; everyone is held accountable for student performance; delegate authority to those with expertise; develop a burning focus on student achievement; create a community of learners in every school; and allow families school choice.

As we pursue CSR, we can see clearly that issues of power and privilege contribute to the continuation of poor schooling for many children, and the effects of racism and classism cannot be ignored. We must continue our conversation about how we can create policies and reform measures that enable schools to teach all students equally well.

Should the task before us include the restructuring of our entire public educational system? I don't mean tinkering; I don't mean piecemeal changes or even well-intentioned reforms. I mean the total restructuring of our schools.

Despite the diversity of American life and inequities arising from local control of schools, many observers have noted how much alike most of our schools are. Have you ever noticed that the office is usually the first thing one sees, the quietest and best-outfitted part of the school, a forbidding place with its long, high counter separating the office staff from others who enter? Long, clear corridors of egg-crate classrooms are broken by banks of lockers and an occasional tidy bulletin board. Classrooms look alike, with teachers' desks at the front or back of each room commanding rows of smaller desks for students. The teachers work independently, their time and efforts managed by periodic bells and announcements boomed by the loudspeaker. Occasional faculty meetings ensure that further announcements are shared.

Schools that have undergone some reform programs and are successfully reinventing teaching and learning look quite different. The office is often difficult to find, stashed away in a corner, full of desks and curriculum materials that mark working spaces for both teachers and administrators. Students and parents enter comfortably with questions and announcements of their own; the place belongs to them, too. Symbolically, office, hallway, and classroom walls are plastered with student work: writing samples, designs, models, and artwork are everywhere. Classrooms have clusters of desks or tables, and teachers' desks may not exist. Handmade models of planets or skeletons hang from the ceiling. Graphs, charts, explanations, questions, and classroom contributions by students adorn walls. Teachers frequently work in teams. Classrooms and hallways are busy! Communication occurs.

This is also part of school reform. The major challenge is to develop policies that support learner-centered and learning-centered practice that attends both to the needs of diverse students and the demands of challenging content. A set of interlocking initiatives is needed. The school environment is a huge piece of reform.

Comprehensive school reform must include the physical environment of the school, curriculum policies focused on defining core concepts and critical skills students need to learn, and assessment practices that ensure that what is being measured emphasizes genuine performance on tasks of true value. In addition, teachers must include high levels of academics for all students and make sure understanding is addressed. We need teacher evaluation that supports as well as encourages active, lifelong learning. Finally, we must create a cohesive community steeped in accountability.

The agenda for comprehensive reform is an ambitious one. It is exceedingly difficult work that takes years of struggle and setbacks. But the rewards will be reaped at every step along the way with every child who experiences greater accomplishment and the ability to contribute to the lives of others.

CSR is expanding rapidly because many models have established development and dissemination infrastructures for replicating and supporting implementations across numerous schools. In other words, the developers can transport their CSR models to schools across the United States, help local educators understand the tenets of the reform, and teach them how to implement the school organization and classroom instruction that the model suggests. In every case, the developers provide some type of initial training or orientation to help educators to at least understand the underlying philosophy of the model. In many circumstances, though, replication also involves a more specific blueprint for implementing and sustaining the model. Highly specified models often prescribe new curricular materials, new methods of instruction, alternative staffing configurations, and a series of ongoing professional development activities.

In addition to the replicable nature of many of the models, expansion of school reform has been fueled by standards-based reform, new federal regulation regarding Title I funds, and the establishment of development corporations like New American Schools to support schoolwide educational programs in high-poverty schools. Only since the mid-1990s has the idea of schoolwide reform emerged as a prominent strategy for helping improve the outcomes of at-risk students from high-poverty schools.

At no time can we suggest that schools and policymakers dismiss promising programs before knowing their potential effects. Instead we must challenge the developers and the educational research community to make a long-term commitment to research-proven comprehensive reform and to establish a marketplace of scientifically-based models capable of bringing reform to the nation's schools.

As I have stated, there are many complications that make our educational mission difficult. Today's focus on accountability takes many teachers away from learning issues. So does the spotlight on test results and the corollary judging and ranking of schools and students. So does the omnipresent quest for *all* students to meet *all* standards in much the same way.

I believe that we—teachers, parents, guardians of rising generations—can have the schools we really want if we are bold enough to look beyond the old myths about what a good school is and instead focus on facilitating intellectual, ethical, and aesthetic growth in our students and ourselves.

Schools are for learners already living a life, not preparing to live a life. The lives they are presently living must be honored.

Our children will not be educated unless the entire nation recognizes and acts to reform our schools. The crisis is upon all of us. Family, government, higher education, and the business world must assist in reforming our schools. Unless we do so our prospects are dim, our nation weakened, our democracy diminished, and our future limited.

4

School Reform Models

Sooner or late, it is ideas, not vested interests, which are dangerous for good or evil.

—John Maynard Keynes

Educators, researchers, foundations, and corporations have long been interested and involved in improving our nation's public schools. Since the 1970s, many of these education stakeholders have developed school reform models to test their ideas about the kinds of organizational, curricular, and instructional changes that help schools to provide a better education for their students.

As a result of the nationwide standards-based accountability movement, policymakers and the public have additional information with which to identify schools that are performing below the standards set for them. Under increased public scrutiny and pressure, many low-performing schools are seeking ways to improve the education they offer to their students. Some, either by choice or mandate, are implementing school reform models as a means of doing so.

The mission and structure of each school reform model reflects the people, time, and context under which it was developed. Models have gotten their starts in a variety of ways. Developers are university researchers, foundations, companies, private organizations, government, districts, individual schools, or a combination of any of these.

While they may have started in different ways, most reform models share some common ground. School reform models are meant to improve education, and often they attempt to do this by stepping away from the traditional ways of thinking about school organization and decision making, staffing, teaching, curriculum, student services, and relationships with parents, business, and the community. School reform models tend to target schools that serve disadvantaged students, though this is not a hard and fast rule.

While there are similarities, there are also major differences among school reform models. For example, some models are appropriate for a specific type or size of school or for certain grade levels, while others can be applied to any school or any size in any location. Some models focus on reforming a particular aspect of the school, such as curriculum. Others call for a wholesale rethinking of the school's organization and operation.

Many school reform models evolve over time as developers learn from experience, address a fluid educational landscape, and respond to the changing needs of students and communities. Some models may start out by reforming a particular aspect of the school, such as the reading curriculum, and then evolve into whole-school reform. Others might initially develop principles around whole-school reform to which a school must adhere and then later develop specific strategies or curricula to realize these principles.

Among reform models that might be labeled whole-school reform, some have a rigid structure and prescribe the curricula, materials, and instructional strategies to be used, while others do not prescribe any of the above but rather have a philosophy of school change, which school staff adopt and apply based on their local situations and needs.

Because school reform models evolve over time, evaluating their effectiveness is a more complicated endeavor than meets the eye. A reform model's objectives may look different today than they did at inception. This is a result of developers' new interests, emerging educational theory and research, or changing student needs. With our current focus on accountability in this era of standards-based reform, these models are now required to demonstrate, with data, their impact on student achievement. Many school reform model developers today are concerned that evaluations conducted by external evaluators often focus on test score data, which may not capture the accomplishments the models have made toward their core objectives.

In addition, evaluating an evolving school reform model can be challenging because perspectives on program evaluation itself changed dramatically in the late 1990s and early 2000s. Traditionally, evaluation has been concerned with inputs and implementation. These are still considered important pieces of evaluation, as they can provide schools with information on the best practices for implementing certain models at their schools. However, evaluation questions around implementation have been overshadowed in recent years by the focus on outcomes, such as student test scores.

Thus, to fairly evaluate a model's effectiveness over time, it is important to look at what the model was trying to accomplish and the progress it made toward its goals based on the standards of the day and the available knowledge and tools of the time.

Beyond assessing an evaluation's rigor and the types of measures it uses, readers of evaluations should keep in mind the following information about the model itself: when it was developed and who developed it along with the primary objectives of the model, and if and how the objectives may have changed to reflect new education movements, such as standards-based reform, address new concerns, such as achievement gap issues, and respond to new policies, such as the federal government's Comprehensive School Reform project.

Many schools do not implement just one model but a combination of models. A school might use one curricular model for reading and another for math plus a whole-school reform model targeted at restructuring leadership and decision-making processes at the school. Hybrids are created at schools to best suit their local needs, to address their weaknesses, and to take advantage of their existing strengths. This hybridization often makes it difficult to attribute change to one particular model. Other reforms at schools, such as the implementation of new local, state, or federal policies, introduce additional variables that serve to further complicate evaluations.

Educators and local policymakers who are considering the adoption of specific school reform models as a strategy to help them improve student achievement and test scores should seek out and read any evaluations or studies available about the models under consideration. If possible, they should speak directly with the model's developers and the evaluation researchers to see what evidence is available for the potential impact on student achievement.

Standards-based reform has dominated the educational policy agendas of both federal and state governments since the late 1990s. In fact, receipt of much federal funding, such as Title I, is now contingent upon schools teaching to state academic standards and measuring student achievement against those standards with statewide, standardized achievement tests. Schools are tapping into school reform models as resources to help them to address these new standards and requirements. Technical assistance offered by model developers helps participating schools maximize the contribution of these models toward meeting new academic goals and standards.

There is a lot of work involved in reforming your school. Before you begin, make some observations of your current program, look at collected data, and most of all spend time asking yourself, "What do we want to change?" How good is your school? Take a walk through your building. Is the school clean? Does the security guard greet you warmly? Are parents in the building? Are the kids smiling? What do you notice when you first enter a classroom? Look for books everywhere; no rows of desks; learning by touching, doing, and researching; visual stimulation; coziness; warmth;

and security. What are the students doing? Do you see relationships, conversation, and teachers among the children, or is the teacher in front of the class? Does the classroom belong to the students or the teacher? Does the teacher individualize, giving each student what he or she needs? Is there multitasking going on? Master teachers are multitaskers. Is your program custom designed or is it one-size-fits-all?

Next, ask yourself, "What do good schools look like?" In good schools, teachers know their students well, curriculum is intellectually challenging and engaging, student voices are encouraged and heard, real-world learning takes place, there is an emotional support system in place, there are close ties with parents, and the school provides a safe and respectful environment.

Consider your observations and look at models of good schools before you tackle the awesome job of reforming your school.

Schoolwide programs are built on the assumption that every aspect of the school's instructional system can and will challenge all students academically. The most successful schools begin with research-based models and rely on their staff to decide how to alter curriculum and instruction to accommodate students' strengths and needs.

Teachers make comprehensive changes, avoiding add-ons or simply replicating standard models. They change their curriculum and teaching strategies by introducing intensive reading and mathematics instruction and reinforcing learning through social studies, science, and the arts. Upgraded instruction for students has these characteristics: consistent use of systematic, research-based teaching strategies; interdisciplinary teaching, exploration, writing, and problem solving around content themes; use of technology as research or writing tools and as the basis of mathematical and scientific exploration; emphasis on building student self-concept, cultural pride, and community identity; and expanded learning opportunities, including early childhood intervention, extended school days, or before- and after-school intensive reading and mathematics programs.

Plans and strategies differ, but the most effective schools often adopt the instructional approaches used by teachers of gifted and talented students, challenge and individualism, modifying services to accommodate the individual circumstances of students who are homeless or come from migrant families, homes where English is not spoken, and communities of color, especially American Indian communities. Often a tutor, a specialist, or a parent works with students within their regular classes. Some students attend special classes, after-school intercession, or summer programs to extend and deepen the quality of the basic instruction they receive. Improved educational resources, aligned with updated academic standards, are essential, as are modern curricula, textbooks, computers, scientific and mathematical tools, and technology.

In other words, schools commit to the success of all students in every academic subject. When necessary, they provide extra assistance to students who experience difficulty mastering any of the state's standards. Interdisciplinary teaching is a common theme; technology connects the classroom with new research, writing, and publication tools. For example, an elementary school in Winter Haven, Florida, organized all of its instruction around thematic units. Children study culture, civilization, history, and geography by researching and writing about the respective contributions that their own cultures have made to civilization.

A big challenge for schoolwide programs will be to overcome reliance on computers for drill and practice of basic skills and learn to use them substantively. Technology centers can be created, where computers, CD-ROMs, DVDs, laser disc players, fax machines, and video adapters are among the routine instructional tools teachers rely on. With networked computers, access to the Internet, and a library of research tools and production software, teachers see the range of instructional opportunities technology offers. In kindergarten and first-grade classrooms, students read and write stories with computers, extending their understanding of how verbal language translates into written text. Upper-grade students hone their research skills with electronic research tools and word processing programs that enable them to conduct sophisticated studies and create formal presentations of their findings. Technology-savvy teachers with knowledge in the disciplines guide students to take advantage of the full capacity of modernized equipment and learning resources. They have the know-how to install and maintain computerized research and reference databases and to help students learn to use the available information to its fullest extent.

Building self-concept and cultural pride is an important component of schoolwide reform. Schools that celebrate the cultural influences in their community instill in students the pride and confidence they need to become competent achievers. Schools that make room for each student's individuality take time to embed what is to be learned into a familiar vernacular so that students can enrich their learning through a context they know.

At Atchison Middle School in Atchison, Kansas, students have online pen pals in California, New York, and Florida. As participants in Scrapbook, USA, a writing project hosted by AOL, these students exchange essays with students in partner schools to learn about different cultures, cities, and schools through the eyes of their peers. Atchison's students have highlighted their online activities in student-produced videos that are screened on the local cable television station.

A middle school (charter) in St. Paul, Minnesota, has developed a community project that hones students' computer skills through a weekly visit by senior citizens who come to the school for student-led computer training. Students show the seniors how to access and browse the Internet and how to use Internet features, such as scanning photos and graphics into their messages.

Curricula, instruction, and schoolwide activities at J. S. Chick Elementary School in Kansas City, Missouri, focus on building students' self-concept as learners and community members through cultural and racial pride. The school's principal emphasizes the importance of teaching students, 985 of whom are African American, to see themselves at the center of society, rather than as outsiders looking in. Teachers organize the core curriculum into thematic units that correspond to African principles such as unity, self-determination, creativity, and collective work and responsibility. Within each unit, students' academic work in every subject is infused with explorations of the contributions of African and African American cultures.

Schoolwide programs often increase the amount and quality of learning time by providing an extended school year or before- and after-school and summer programs. Before- and after-school programs and summer academies can provide students year-round exploratory opportunities that develop the knowledge they need to achieve state standards. At McNair Elementary School in North Charleston, South Carolina, one hundred students in grades K–3 who scored poorly on the district's tests spent six weeks during the summer studying science, including space, marine life, and conservation, all topics they would be tested on during the school year. Weekly field trips engaged students in hands-on learning.

One new approach is called a parallel school, separated from traditional schools and would-be schedules by being held after hours. This type of school provides services such as counseling, driver education, drug abuse programs, and after-school supports.

Satellite schools are another type of public school and are located within buildings that house large businesses or corporations. The purpose is to encourage bonding between schools and businesses.

Gradeless classes, in which elementary students are grouped by ability rather than age, have been in existence in some Kentucky schools since 1990. Personalized curriculum allowing independent educational programs/plans for each student is becoming more popular. High-tech learning is becoming increasingly available as educational programs are able to use computerized programs to create lesson plans and track student progress.

SCHOOL REFORM MODELS

Choices in school reform models are available from many sources. The following are examples of tools for schools.

Schoolwide Enrichment Model

The Schoolwide Enrichment Model is based upon a vision that schools are places for talent development. The model uses the pedagogy of gifted education to make school more challenging and enjoyable for all students. The model provides the flexibility for each school to develop its own unique program in accordance with local resources, student population, and faculty interests and strengths. Two major objectives of the model include providing a broad range of advanced-level enrichment experiences for all students and using student responses to these experiences as stepping stones for relevant follow-up. The model's roots in gifted education programs is indeed a positive feature, because such programs, unencumbered by prescribed curricular and instructional methods, have proven to be a fertile ground for experimentation with school improvement concepts.

Bringing the Schoolwide Enrichment Model to large segments of the school population requires three essential elements.

- Total Talent Portfolio: Students complete and contribute their best work samples to reflect their strengths and interests as learners. This focuses on students' strengths rather than their defects and is used by schools to decide which talent development opportunities to offer individual students.
- Curriculum Modification Techniques: The model encourages the development of a challenging curriculum, and one that injects both in-depth and enrichment learning experiences into regular school activities. Curriculum modification can be done through textbook analysis, elimination of repetitive or previously mastered material, provision of time for enrichment, the expansion of the depth of learning, and an emphasis on students' roles as firsthand investigators.
- Enrichment Learning and Teaching: The development of the school program should be based upon the principles that each learner is unique, learning is more effective when students enjoy what they are doing, the content relates to real life, and the goal is to have the students apply knowledge and skills through their own construction of meaning.

The Schoolwide Enrichment Model can operate within three types of school structures. The model is to enhance rather than replace the regular curriculum, through modification. Enrichment clusters are multiage groups of students who meet regularly with a facilitator to share and pursue a common interest. Clusters, which revolve around major disciplines, interdisciplinary themes, or crossdisciplinary topics, emphasize the development of higher-order thinking skills and the creative and productive application of these skills to real-world situations. A continuum of special services, supplementary services including individual or small-group counseling, mentor relationships, and direct assistance in facilitating advanced-level work, is essential for a talent development program to be effective in meeting the needs of individual students.

Change should be initiated, nurtured, and monitored within each school using the model. It does not replace existing school structures, but seeks to improve them by concentrating on internal and external factors that have a direct bearing on learning. The procedure for adoption and implementation of the model calls for ownership by and involvement of staff, administration, and parents. Implementation steps include team building led by those familiar with the model, a decision to embrace the model concepts, and the development of a mission statement for the school. The formation of a Schoolwide Enrichment Team to guide the implementation of the model is essential.

The Schoolwide Enrichment Model is a product of fifteen years of research and field testing. The model has been implemented in school districts worldwide, and extensive evaluations and research studies indicate the model's effectiveness. (Contact the National Research Center on Gifted and Talented at the University of Connecticut for further information.) The model suggests that all students, including low-income students, need to be provided with challenging and accelerated learning content. Learning experiences are therefore designed with the goal of engaging and offering stimulation and enjoyment to all students.

Enrichment Clusters

Enrichment clusters, mentioned briefly earlier in the chapter, merit further exploration. Enrichment clusters are groups of students who share common interests and who come together during specially designed time blocks to pursue these interests. The main rationale for participation in one or more clusters is that students and teachers want to be there. All teachers and teacher aides are involved in organizing the cluster, and numerous schools have also involved parents and other community members. Everything that students do in the cluster is directed toward completing a product or delivering a service for a real-world audience.

The concept of enrichment learning and teaching evolved from the Enrichment Triad Model. In this model, students are exposed to a variety of topics and areas of study not covered in the regular curriculum, learning how-to-learn skills (written, oral, visual) and firsthand investigation of real problems. The enrichment model is based on ways in which people learn in a natural environment.

Clusters are offered for an extended time block, usually ninety minutes to three hours per week. Students enter a cluster based on interests and other information gleaned from a Total Talent Portfolio. The enrichment clusters revolve around major disciplines, interdisciplinary themes, or crossdisciplinary topics. A theatrical/television production group, for example, might include actors, writers, technical specialists, and costume designers. Student work is directed toward producing a product or service, and the clusters deal with how-to knowledge, thinking skills, and interpersonal relations that apply in the real world. Instead of lesson plans or unit plans, three key questions guide learning: What do people with an interest in this area do? What knowledge, materials, and other resources are needed? In what ways can the product or service be used to affect the intended audience?

The model is implemented in several steps: access the interests of students and staff, create a schedule, locate staff to facilitate cluster, provide an orientation for facilitators so the clusters do not become minicourses or traditional teacher-directed experiences, prepare cluster descriptions and register students, and celebrate your success by exhibiting projects, providing public relations, and bringing media attention to student products.

Research on enrichment clusters conducted in ethnically diverse, low-socioeconomic urban schools indicates that the gifted education pedagogy could be successfully used to challenge all students in these schools. Parents were extremely supportive, as were teachers and students. Attendance was better on the days on which clusters were held.

The enrichment clusters model is designed based on the research suggesting that instruction must take into account the varying abilities, background interests, experiences, and learning styles of each student. The student is able to showcase his or her talents in a variety of ways. Learning is more meaningful when content and process are learned within the context of a real problem, when students use authentic methods to address the problem, and when there is a tangible outcome. Finally, the model builds on research suggesting that low-income students and students of color need to be provided with challenging and accelerated learning content. In enrichment clusters, students work together with teachers and others on activities in which they have a strong interest, drawing on those skills and talents which can contribute to success with the product or outcome.

Families and Schools Together (FAST)

Families and Schools Together (FAST) is a two-year, school-based, elementary program that builds bonds, trust, and supportive networks for families and children; increases parent involvement with children both at school and home; and increases resiliency, attention span, and readiness to learn in elementary school children.

FAST uses a highly structured activity-based approach to promote the development of school-parent-community-child partnerships. The curriculum is designed to enhance parent-child interactions, empower parents, and build parent support groups.

The FAST program was developed to address many of the problems faced by elementary schools with significant numbers of students with low achievement. The program was designed around emerging research indicating that partnerships between schools, communities, and parents could prevent the school-related performance and behavioral problems of low-income children.

The program was developed in 1988 and began in the Madison, Wisconsin, school district with support from Family Service America, a national organization whose membership includes a large number of community-based counseling and family support agencies. At this time, the program can be found in a variety of culturally diverse school communities in twenty-six states. It is working in urban inner-city schools as well as at isolated, rural school sites.

To join the FAST program, a school must identify and partner with two community-based agencies, such as a mental health agency and a substance abuse agency, who agree to work with the school over a period of two years. Three professionals, one from the school and one from each of the partner agencies, are identified and trained through the Family Services America National Replication Center. Participating children and parents gather once a week for eight sessions at the school. The eight sessions usually take place around an evening meal. Following the sessions, monthly support meetings are designed to maintain an active social network.

The activities at each session are lively and fun and build a sense of family unity. In fifteen minutes of uninterrupted quality time, parents play one-on-one with the child in ways that build the child's self-esteem and enhance family communication. Parents are also given time to build an information support network for themselves to help each other discover solutions to parenting and family concerns.

Evaluations of FAST at the schools where it has been implemented indicate positive outcomes. Behavior both at home and at school improves. Parents are also much more active in school events than they were previously.

The FAST program is currently operating in extremely isolated rural areas of northern California, northern Wisconsin, and Iowa, as well as in inner-city neighborhoods in Chicago, New Orleans, Los Angeles, and Washington, DC. The program has also been implemented in school communities with families where the first language is not English (Vietnamese families, American Indians on certain reservations, newly arrived Hispanic families, and African immigrant families).

FAST draws on research from a number of behavioral science disciplines, including social work, family therapy, child psychiatry, and child and family psychology. The program also blends in knowledge emerging from research in such other fields as delinquency and substance abuse prevention, prevention of domestic and other forms of violence, parent involvement in education, and family support. FAST makes use of many ideas, clinical practices, and research that have been used successfully for years by social work practitioners.

Community for Learning Program (CFL)

The Community for Learning (CFL) program is a broad-based, school-family-community coordinated approach to improving student learning. The major premise of this school-based intervention program is that the national standards of educational outcomes can and must be upheld for all students, including those who are "at the margins." A centerpiece for the CFL program is an integrated design framework for a collaborative process of finding ways to harness all the resources, expertise, and energies in linking schools with other learning environments, including homes, churches, libraries, public- and private-sector workplaces, and postsecondary institutions, to support the learning of each student.

There is a growing demand for educational reforms to improve schools' capacity to more effectively and efficiently serve all students, including those from educationally and economically disadvantaged backgrounds, by providing inclusive and coordinated education and related services. The quality of life available to these children and families is threatened by a perilous set of modern morbidities that often involve poverty, lack of employment opportunities, disorderly and stressful environments, poor health care, children born to children, and highly fragmented patterns of service. CFL seeks to unite the resources and expertise of the school, the family, and the community in fostering educational resilience and the learning success of inner-city children and youth.

The implementation of CFL is supported by a delivery system that provides organizations and professional development support at the school and classroom levels. The program includes the Schoolwide Reform Development component to assist in service delivery, the Family-Community Support Component to link the resources and energies of families and the community to support student learning, and the Adaptive Learning Environment Model to meet the diverse needs of individual students in regular classroom settings, including special education, Title I, and bilingual students.

The CFL program design consists of components that address the learning needs of the students, administration support requirements for achieving a high degree of program implementation, and the staff development needs of the school and related service providers. These components include a site-specific implementation plan, a staff development program, development of student self-responsibility for behavior and learning, an individualized learning plan for each student, one-on-one tutoring based on individual needs, and a school-linked comprehensive, coordinated health and human services delivery program that focuses on the wellness and learning success of each student.

Implementation of CFL focuses on site-specific planning that includes a comprehensive needs assessment involving all stakeholder groups followed by planning and implementation of the program by school-based personnel, families, and community agencies.

The specific design of the program to be implemented at each CFL school site is based on the information obtained from the comprehensive needs assessment. Design decisions to be made at the building level include how the resources identified during the needs assessment will be used, modified, and reallocated for effective implementation.

The CFL program seeks to impact three major areas of student outcomes: improved student achievement, patterns of active learning consistent with classroom practices, and positive attitudes by students and staff toward their school learning environment.

Students in CFL schools tend to have a higher level of aspiration for academic learning, have better behavior, and show a positive pattern in changes in math and reading scores. Data also showed that families and the community became increasingly active in a wide range of school activities.

The development of the Community for Learning program was influenced by over two decades of research and field-based implementation of innovative school programs. In particular, it draws from the research base on fostering educational resilience of children and youth beset by multiple, co-occurring risks and from restructuring programs that focus on school organization and instructional delivery in ways that are responsive to the development of and learning needs of the individual child. The model also draws upon research regarding connections among school, family, and community. At the core of the CFL program is a coordinated approach to service delivery that calls for shared responsibility among collaborative teams of school-based professionals and related service and community agencies and the forging of close connections with the family and the community.

Success for All

Success for All is a structured whole-school reform model focusing on students in grades prekindergarten through grade six. The model is designed to raise the achievement of students in low-performing schools. The idea behind Success for All is to use everything known from research on effective instruction for students in low-performing schools to prevent and intervene in the development of learning problems in the early years. A principal thrust is to ensure that every child in the school succeeds in learning to read at grade level by the end of third grade. A bilingual version of the program has also been developed.

Success for All grew out of a partnership between Baltimore City Public Schools and what is now the Center for Research in Education of Students Placed At Risk at Johns Hopkins University. It has been implemented in more than one thousand schools in thirty-seven states throughout the country.

Specific elements of the program include reading, writing, and language arts offered daily for ninety minutes, with students regrouped by reading level across age lines; cooperative learning that drives the curriculum and emphasis placed on individual accountability, common goals, and recognition of team success; tutors working one-on-one with any student failing to keep up; facilitators working with teachers to help the reading program; eight-week assessments; and a family support team, comprised of the principal, facilitator, social workers, and parents, to help ensure the success of the program.

All teachers receive a detailed teacher's manual supplemented by three days of in-service at the beginning of the school year provided by project trainers who observe classrooms, meet with teachers, and conduct in-service presentations on such topics as classroom management, instructional pace, and cooperative learning.

There has been strong evidence that the program clearly increases reading performance, especially for students who perform in the lowest 25 percent of their class. The longer the program is in existence, the higher the reading performance among students. Success for All has been implemented successfully in schools with tremendously diverse student populations. It is being employed by schools with high numbers of African American students, schools that are predominantly Hispanic (both natives and immigrants to this country), schools with large numbers of Asian students, and integrated schools. The model is being used in inner-city schools in several large cities across the country as well as in a broad range of rural schools.

The Success for All model is predicated on research evidence stressing the importance of early academic success and incorporates a number of prevention and intervention strategies designed to ensure all children develop a strong foundation in reading by the third grade. There is a strong emphasis on school readiness and the development of prereading skills at the preschool level, which is critical for school success for low-income children, many of whom do not have the opportunity to develop these skills prior to starting school.

In the early elementary grades, Success for All focuses relentlessly on providing ample time and resources for children to gain strong skills in reading by the third grade. The intention here is to prevent students from being retained in grade or placed in special education programs or remedial education. Research suggests that these traditional "remedies" to poor performance in reading have little or no positive effect on student achievement. The Success for All curriculum makes generous use of cooperative learning, which has proved itself to be effective in strengthening students' academic as well as social skills. The Success for All staff development component is consistent with research on adult learning indicating that professional development should be focused and provide for frequent follow-up.

Adaptive Learning Environments Model (ALEM)

The Adaptive Learning Environments Model (ALEM) is an innovative educational program designed to meet the diverse social and academic needs of students in regular classes. A product of over two decades of research, development, and school-based implementation in a variety of communities, the model serves as an alternative approach to educational reform for schools striving to be responsive to the learning needs of individual students with varying abilities, experiences, and socioeconomic backgrounds.

Underlying the model's design is the premise that students learn in different ways and at varying rates and require different amounts of instructional support. The ALEM accommodates and builds upon these differences through adaptive instruction, in which a variety of instructional methods are adapted and tailored to the needs and learning characteristics of individual students, and specific interventions are used to increase each student's ability to benefit from the learning environment.

The call for programs that work for the educational success of each student, including those with special needs and those who are considered to be academically at risk, has become a central issue in school reform programs. There have been significant advances in theory and practical knowledge of effective instruction, and growing evidence suggests a great variability in the ways that students acquire, organize, retain, and generate knowledge and skills. The ALEM was designed to cull from the knowledgebase on what makes teaching and learning more effective and efficient.

The ALEM's goal is to ensure achievement of basic academic skills and other valued educational outcomes, including students' positive self-perceptions of their academic and social competence, sense of responsibility for their own education and the broader community, and competencies in coping with the social and academic demands of schooling. In order to accomplish this, the model focuses on systematically integrating features that theory, research, and practice have shown to be instructionally effective and pedagogically meaningful.

Implementation of the ALEM is supported by delivery of adaptive instruction in regular classroom settings, classroom management and program implementation, and school- and district-level interventions.

Effective implementation of the model requires teachers to use all forms of knowledge in implementing effective classroom practices to accommodate students' diverse learning needs. Although adaptive instruction calls for individualized planning, teachers do not work with students on a one-on-one basis. Whole-class and small-group instruction and peer-based cooperative learning are incorporated when suited for achieving certain intended student outcomes or ways to improve instructional efficiency.

In the ALEM classroom, individual differences are viewed as the norm rather than the exception. While teachers, parents, and the students themselves recognize differences in rates of progress, the acquisition of basic academic skills and the development of social competence and self-esteem are expected of each student. Under the ALEM program, specialist teachers (e.g., reading specialists funded under Title I or special education teachers) and other related service professionals (e.g., speech pathologists or school psychologists) work with regular classroom teachers in a coordinated system of instructional and related service delivery.

The ALEM is designed to provide instruction that is responsive to student needs and to provide school staff with ongoing professional development and school-based program implementation support to achieve student success. Implementation features the following design elements: individualized progress plans, featuring student self-direction and problem-solving ability along with social and personal development to enhance student academic success; assessment to ensure student mastery; classroom management, focusing on student self-responsibility; professional development that provides ongoing training and technical assistance; a school-based restructuring process that provides school and classroom organizational support; and an active family involvement program that is targeted to support student learning success.

When a high degree of implementation is achieved, a unique classroom scenario is created. Students can be found working in virtually every area of the classroom engaging in a variety of learning activities, including participating in small-group instruction, receiving one-on-one tutoring, or engaging in peer-based collaboration activities. Teachers circulate among the students, instructing and providing corrective feedback. The teacher bases instruction on diagnostic test results and informal assessments. Every student is expected to make steady progress in meeting the curricular standards. Learning tasks are broken down into incremental steps, providing frequent opportunities for evaluation.

In classrooms where a high degree of implementation is achieved, teachers tend to spend more time on instruction than on managing students, and students tend to be highly task oriented. Steady and productive interaction between teachers and students and among students replaces the passive learning mode typically found in conventional classrooms. Interaction among students, for the most part, focuses on sharing ideas and working together on learning tasks. Distracted behavior on the part of individual students is minimal and does not seem to interfere with the work of others.

Adaptive education approaches to improve student learning outcomes have been noted by researchers and practitioners as a promising alternative approach for accommodating the diverse learning needs of individual students, including those with exceptional talents and those with special needs. Implementing adaptive education strategies as an alternative approach to improving student outcomes can be traced back to the early 1900s as a part of the progressive education movement in this country. Changes in the conceptualization of individual differences and the growing research base in developmental and cognitive psychology have resulted in increasing attention to individual differences in how learning takes place and what influences learning. Individual differences in learning are no longer considered static, but can be modified either before the instructional process begins or as part of the actual process.

Urban Learner Framework

The Urban Learner Framework is an integrated knowledge base that incorporates and disseminates the most current, promising, and pertinent research concerned with improving and restructuring schools in urban districts. This knowledge base has been organized into a decision-making framework challenging the sweeping generalizations that have envisioned the urban learner as deprived, underachieving, unmotivated, and at risk. It presents a new vision of the urban learner as culturally diverse, capable, effortful, and resilient, and represents a major paradigm shift in research and theories of intelligence and learning.

The power and usefulness of the Urban Learner Framework comes from its integration of research knowledge into a coherent focus for developing strategies. Because the framework's vision is integrated, it helps to reduce the fragmentation produced by reforms that deal solely with organizational processes or with aspects of pedagogy. Internalizing the principles of the framework enables educational communities to explore new meanings, examine current practices, focus leadership, develop context-specific strategies, and expand accountability. The Urban Learner Framework utilizes four research-based themes for decision making within the community and school setting.

The four research themes are described as follows: cultural and linguistic diversity and learning, in which teachers are encouraged to connect with learners' cultural experiences, emphasizing how culture plays a major role in all human development; unrecognized abilities and underdeveloped potential, in which the belief that each child possesses a different combination of natural talents across the range of intelligences that include leadership, math, art, music, and organization is focused; enhancing ability development through motivation and effort under positive, supportive conditions; and resilience, which is developed through caring and supportive teachers along with an accelerated curriculum built on high expectations.

The Urban Learner Framework helps urban educators determine appropriate curriculum, instruction, and assessment; design staff development programs; and, most of all, establish supportive school environments building visionary leadership and effective management.

This framework has been introduced in districts and schools throughout the country. Staff is introduced to examples of what the Urban Learner Framework looks like in practice, an action plan is developed, professional development is ongoing, and an evaluation plan is created.

Districts using the framework have seen the development of more positive attitudes among children and staff. The framework also serves as a bridge between research and educational practice. It has consistently received strong positive evaluations from audiences of educators, from parents, from districts, and from schools when used as a guide for designing and implementing systemic change.

Recent theories of intelligence, learning, and instruction suggest that the four themes (cultural and linguistic diversity, unrecognized abilities and underdeveloped potential, enhancing ability through motivation and effort, and resilience), when taken together, generate a vision of urban learners as culturally diverse, capable, motivated, and resilient. The Urban Learner Framework draws on findings from a variety of research areas: anthropology, psychology, and sociology, which highlight the fundamental role that culture plays in all human development; cognitive research, which suggests intelligence is able to be modified, and that each child possesses a unique combination of natural talents across the range of many different intelligences; research on other cultures, which indicates that academic achievement is more likely when students believe that effort will lead to success; and research that suggests that urban learners are more likely to eschew the dangers of the inner city, such as gangs, drugs, and violence, when they are provided with caring, challenging, and meaningful educational experiences.

School Change Model

The School Change Model is an approach to schoolwide reform that aims at improving achievement and other student outcomes by creating a coherent and focused schoolwide effort: although it was developed in a predominantly Latino school with an existing bilingual education program, the model's principles are probably equally applicable in other situations. The model does not describe a specific instructional program. Rather, it identifies four key "change elements" that educators can use to help bring about positive changes in teaching and learning at a school: goals that are set and shared, indicators that measure success, assistance by capable others, and leadership that supports and pressures.

The School Change Model was the result of a collaborative project between a university researcher and an elementary school principal who wanted to improve student achievement at a predominantly Latino school, Freeman Elementary School in Los Angeles. The model is currently used mainly in the Los Angeles Unified School District, but is spreading to other metropolitan areas.

The process begins with teachers and leadership setting shared, specific learning goals and expectations for students in chosen academic areas. It continues with the development and analysis of key indicators of student achievement in relation to the goals. The indicators can include, for example, grade-level designation of reading texts that students are reading, performance-based assessment, or standardized achievement measures. Teachers sustain the change process in groups, routinely and jointly studying lessons and examining student work and indicators of achievement (teacher groups focus on learning and exploring better teaching methods to help accomplish schoolwide goals and evaluating the effects of ongoing efforts). Supportive and pressuring leadership maintains focus and momentum.

A critical concept is the setting, which is defined as any instance in which two or more people come together in a new relationship over a sustained period of time in order to achieve certain goals. School improvement takes place in specific and concrete settings where people meet to create a focused, coherent, and sustained effort to improve student learning. Relative settings include academic expectations, academic assessment, staff meetings, grade-level meetings, teacher work groups, and consultant-principal meetings. All groups plan strategies, address issues, and help coordinate change efforts schoolwide.

There is no implementation infrastructure. Educators use the goals, indicators, assistance, and leadership of each school interested in using this model to promote change. The model also enables educators to create a focused and coherent schoolwide effort aimed at improving student achievement in specific targeted areas of the curriculum. Schools that have adapted the model to fit their needs report that students have matched or surpassed district, state, and national norms. There has also been progress in English reading for the bilingual schools that have used the model. Teachers say that they have worked more collaboratively on schoolwide goals and receive the support and training they need. They also feel that there is a much stronger school-level leadership that has been instrumental in promoting constructive change.

The aim of the School Change Model is to provide overall coherence to a school's effort to improve achievement and other student outcomes. It provides a focus for unifying the different activities and initiatives at the school under a common purpose. The model is derived from the research on effective schools and educational change.

Recent research supports the idea that common and mutually understood goals are vital for successful change efforts. Motivation theory suggests that goal setting matters because goals affect behavior. Indicators of success complement goals by reinforcement. Assistance is also a key to successful change.

The School Change Model places emphasis on presenting information, creating settings that encourage discussion and analysis, and providing opportunities to attempt and reflect upon new behaviors that will assist teachers in accomplishing student learning goals. Finally, leadership is the element most closely associated with efforts to make schools more effective. Together the four change elements listed earlier create a dynamic that can lead to positive changes and improved student outcomes.

Comer School Development Program

Another model I would like to touch on is the Comer School Development Program. This model has a unique focus on developing the whole child. Unlike models with a formulaic approach to curriculum and teaching methods, this holistic strategy links children's academic growth with their emotional wellness and moral development in a collaborative school culture congenial to learning. The program is designed in such a way that life skills and academic performance improve.

Since 1968, when the model was created by James Comer, a Yale University child psychologist, it has been utilized in more than 1150 schools nationwide.

Dr. Comer believes that for various reasons, many inner-city children enter school "underdeveloped": lacking the personal, social, and moral foundations necessary for academic and life success. He also believes that many teachers lack adequate knowledge of child development or an understanding of their students' lives and culture, leaving them unprepared to deal appropriately with these children and their families to effectively foster their learning.

The Comer process puts the responsibility on schools and their principals, administration, teachers, and parents to come together to agree on an action plan for the school, utilizing both social and academic components.

Teachers, principals, and parents make decisions collaboratively, in the best interests of the students. The Comer process guides schools to set up a network of teams to manage the school and to deal with various facets of the social and academic needs of the school.

Under the Comer strategy, a successful school should look and feel like a community center, where parent volunteers are engaged in helping teachers and administration makes key decisions about running the school and providing support for the school community. There is an emphasis on linking the schools with the social services and on ongoing staff development.

According to research on the Comer process in high-poverty and high-minority urban settings, the strategy has been very effective at improving student achievement when implemented conscientiously and consistently over a period of five years or more.

When you walk in the door of a Comer school you will see management teams using collaborative decision-making and consensus, emphasis on holistic child development, parent volunteers who are welcomed and seen in a variety of important functions within the school, and a social worker to assist children and help manage the implementation of the Comer process in the school environment.

Research and evaluation on the Comer process show that children from all income, geographic, language, and cultural groups can gain the social and academic skills needed to do well in school when the educational enterprise adequately addresses their needs.

Achievement First Model

A final model worth mentioning is the Achievement First Model, founded by Dacia Toll. Achievement First, a nonprofit, operates nine public charter schools (fifteen academies) in Connecticut and New York. Her students, selected by lottery, are 98 percent black and Latino and have consistently made dramatic gains in student achievement. I had the opportunity to hear Dacia Toll speak in Minneapolis, Minnesota, on November 13, 2008, and she said that you focus on "whatever it takes" to provide all students with the academic and character skills they need to graduate from top colleges, succeed in a competitive world, and serve as the next generation of leaders for our communities.

She opened her first school in 1999 with 84 students and has grown to 3700 as of 2008. Core elements of an Achievement First school are unwavering focus on breakthrough student achievement; investment in talent development; focus on instruction, curriculum, and data; more time on task (three hours spent daily on reading in K–2, and 3.5 hours spent daily on reading and writing in grades 3–7); and a disciplined, achievement-oriented school culture.

Evaluation completed by Achievement First shows success in all areas.

Many people outside the educational world don't realize how difficult it really is to know what goes on in a school. Kids stream into the schools in the morning and out in the afternoon, and what goes on inside those buildings is a bit of a mystery to all but those inside, and sometimes to them as well. Parents especially find themselves mystified, particularly when their children respond to questions about what they did that day with the all-purpose phrases "nothing" and "I don't know."

For the most part, schools have not been organized for the purpose of making sure all students learn enough to become productive citizens (to read, write, apply mathematical formulas, understand political and scientific issues enough to vote sensibly, and serve on a jury honorably).

In the past schools were organized in a way that sorted children and then offered them very different kinds of education. Baby boomers will remember the "tracks" that their high schools offered: college prep, business, and vocational. Most school systems have stopped using the word *tracks*, but the sorting practices remain. The premise was simple. Schools serving large numbers of children of poverty or children of color cannot be expected to reach high academic standards, nor can they be expected to be high achieving.

The American public never bought into this. They assumed that the job of schools was to teach all children. Parents and policymakers tired of hearing stories of children who spent twelve or thirteen years in school without ever learning how to read or even use life skills math. The public began to demand that schools demonstrate that they educate children rather than simply house them. Congress told the states that they needed to show results. Before deciding what academic gains should look like, states first had to decide what children should learn. Some states set ambitious goals for their children, some set low goals, and some set no goals. Little progress was made.

The above inconsistencies among the states led to No Child Left Behind (NCLB). The nation declared that schools have the responsibility to teach every child to meet his or her state's standards of learning. To those accustomed to the idea that the job of schools is to sort children rather than to educate them, NCLB has come as a shock. Some teachers, principals, and superintendents around the country have spent years saying the NCLB goals are ridiculous given the types of kids and considering all the different backgrounds and issues they bring into the schools. These voices need to be silenced. It is not ridiculous to expect students to read, write, and use math.

There are schools that are achieving, schools with a significant population of children living in poverty and children of color. These schools have a jump start on the reform initiative and are models worth looking at. These schools are models in practice.

Frankford Elementary School (K–6) in Frankford, Delaware, with a student population of mostly African Americans and Latinos (many recent immigrants from Mexico and children of agricultural workers who themselves had little education), put aside the "reading wars" and chose a plan that assesses each child to get an idea of where the child is and to diagnose any problems in reading. An individual plan is then developed. The child who needs extra work or phonemic awareness, for example, gets it. If a child is reading well, he or she gets additional enrichment in the form of more challenging chapter books. Social studies and science classes become times to read.

University Park Campus School (grades 7–12) in Worcester, Massachusetts, was founded by a partnership between the City of Worcester and Clark University. The school is located in an area of trash-strewn lots bound by chain-link fences, blank storefronts, and low-rise apartments densely packed with three or four families per unit, adding up to twenty to twenty-five people in one place. The population is made up of Eastern European immigrants as well as Latino and Vietnamese families. The students, most of whom arrive at least two or three or even more years behind in reading, all pass the state high school exit exams, most at high levels. All students go on to college. The school offers excellent instruction in a focused college-prep curriculum taught by teachers who know their fields, are convinced all kids can and must learn at high levels, and are willing to support them. They make it seem simple, and it is worth enough to observe and study the program.

Dayton's Bluff Achievement Plus Elementary School (grades K–6) is located in St. Paul, Minnesota. Most of the students are African American or Hmong. The school demonstrates the power that a comprehensive school reform model can have on helping an educational program improve academically. America's Choice was the model used. Writer's workshop, reader's workshop, and math workshop were incorporated into a narrow focus on standards. The Responsive Classroom Behavior Model was also used. Higher rates of proficiency were the result.

The High School of the Recording Arts (HSRA), grades 9–12, is also located in St. Paul, Minnesota. The mission of HSRA is to provide youth the opportunity to achieve a high school diploma through the exploration of the music business and other creative endeavors. The school began as a pilot program developed by Studio 4 Enterprises and through word of mouth. The program grew from 15 students in 1997 to 225 students today. HSRA is a culturally sensitive, project-based, public charter school that operates within and around a professional recording studio. Students gain access to the studio by completing academic projects in core learning areas of English, math, science, and social studies. It also appeals to several students who have dropped out or been expelled from traditional schools and helps these students to complete their high school diploma requirements.

American Indian children often get left out of national education discussions, but as a group they tend to score terribly on state tests. Not so at Lapwai Elementary School (grades K–8) in Lapwai, Idaho. The town is located on the Nez Perce reservation and consists of a supermarket, a gas station, lots of tiny churches, and a few houses. The unemployment rate is high in the area. Eighty-four percent of the students are American Indians who live in the surrounding hills, and the remaining students are white. Lapwai has built a strong foundation of learning by using a coherent curriculum and a culture of collaboration. The tribal council is a major stakeholder and partner in the cultural education of the students. Through culture, reading, math, social studies, and science are project-based enterprises and link the school to the community.

These schools and others like them have shared qualities.

- They teach all students.
- They do not teach to the state tests.
- They have high expectations for all students.
- They embrace and use all the data they can get their hands on.
- They constantly reexamine what they do.
- They embrace accountability.
- They make decisions based on what is good for the kids, not what is good for adults.
- They leverage as many resources from the community as possible.
- They expand the time students, particularly struggling students, have in school by creating before- and after-school classes, summer school, year-round calendars, and extended tutoring.
- They establish an atmosphere of respect.
- The staff genuinely likes the kids.
- Principals are a constant presence, and are important leaders, but not the only leaders.
- They pay attention to the quality of the teaching staff.
- They provide teachers with the time to meet, to plan, to work collaboratively, and to observe each other.
- They think seriously about professional development.
- They carefully acculturate all newly hired teachers.
- They have high-quality, dedicated, and competent office and building staff that feel themselves part of the educational mission of the school.
- They are great and fun places to work.

Another quality comes through as well. These schools have the kind of camaraderie that comes from teams of people facing difficult challenges together, not unlike the camaraderie that is built in military units, sports teams, theatrical groups, and any other group that goes through an arduous process to achieve a common goal. As a result, they do not have the kind of turnover that many schools with similar demographics have. When people leave, for the most part, it is because they retire, or their spouses are transferred, or they are promoted to new positions of leadership, not because they are fleeing to teach elsewhere. Many teachers want to work with children of poverty and children of color if they can work in an environment where they will be helped to become master teachers.

To sum this up, the adults in these schools expect their students to learn and they work hard to master the skills and knowledge necessary to teach those students. The schools profiled here demonstrate that the job of educating kids to high standards, even kids traditionally considered "hard to teach," is theoretically possible. The challenges these schools and others like them have overcome include the ideas that poverty and discrimination are insurmountable barriers to academic achievement; that today's kids are so damaged by television, video games, and hip-hop music that they are impervious to books and scholarship; that good, qualified teachers simply won't work in difficult environments; and that existing teachers and principals are incapable of improvement.

The schools profiled here have proven these arguments wrong. When you overcome poverty and discrimination with enough thoughtful instruction, careful organization, and what can only be recognized as a kind of pigheaded optimism, you get learning. These schools have tackled the theoretical challenges one by one and have proven that those challenges can be conquered.

The question today is not about what works, but about why we do not implement what we know works in all schools for all students.

5

Reinventing the American High School

It takes courage to grow up and turn out to be whom you really are.

—E. E. Cummings

If your high school experience is like most students, you spend seven hours every day at school. The half-hour lunch and time spent with friends may compute as the most intellectually engaging moments you spend, despite the teachers' best intentions. The other six-and-a-half hours, in class and out, are spent working your ass off . . . trying to find a girlfriend or boyfriend, flirting, dispelling rumors about yourself, starting rumors about other people, and all the other things you do to survive high school. The great game of high school is rooted in adult mating rituals and the social reproductions of class hierarchy to a degree that very few parents, teachers, or administrators admit. The game determines your success at school.

Is your high school like the picture above or could it possibly fit the next scenario?

Brian is a ninth grader at a public charter school in Detroit. A year ago, he exhibited the look and behavior of the majority of kids in the city who do not make it to the twelfth grade. He learned little and acted out a lot. Then last spring his teacher discovered that Brian has a talent for mathematics. She quickly enrolled him in a Saturday math program conducted by Wayne State University. He became the star of the math program and came back with a project to share that was worthy of *A Beautiful Mind*. Now he talks about going to college on a math scholarship.

What made the uncovering of Brian's skills possible were his school's small class size and a new one-student-at-a-time approach. This model allows each teacher to shepherd a small group of students, no more than fifteen, throughout their high school careers. The problem is that even after two decades of urban school reform efforts, Brian's school is the exception, not the rule. That is why only 4,600 students are enrolled as seniors in the Detroit Public School system, from a class that began with 15,000 freshmen students four years ago.

The root of the problem appears to lie in a misguided attempt during the last twenty years to reform high schools that are saddled with one-size-fits-all learning strategies, large class sizes, student anonymity, and lack of meaningful student connections to adults in school and in the outside world.

It is long past time for urban education studies to abandon its efforts to make mass standardized high schools work better. Instead it should opt for new, smaller, more professional schools designed to keep kids in class and to prepare them for postsecondary studies.

Today's urban schools are like mass-production factories of the Industrial Age. They usually offer only one learning approach: acquiring skills and information through a textbook while sitting quietly at a desk. Yet this is the preferred learning style of no more than 20 percent of the population. The same material is offered on the same day, in the same way, to each child of similar age regardless of the student's skill level, learning style, maturity, and interests. That is why the mainstays of school reform—more testing, teacher training, longer school days, and smaller class size—have had so little effect.

Community expectations that every student be able to read, write, and enjoy mathematics to certain measurable standards by the end of high school are reasonable and necessary. However, the notion that all kids will achieve these levels at the same time and in the same way results in a forced learning march that breeds failure and dropouts.

Fortunately, a number of urban and nonurban public high schools have been testing replacement models with encouraging results (graduating 90 percent of their students from high school and sending them on to college). While differing in a multitude of ways, these schools possess common innovative features: each student is provided with an enduring one-to-one relationship with an adult in the school, which ensures that there is always a caring teacher who can support him or her; schools are kept small to eliminate anonymity and prevent teens from slipping through the cracks; and learning is individualized by using projects that take into account the individual student's passions and preferred learning styles.

Is this the only promising replacement model for our failing high schools, especially urban high schools? Certainly not. But schools with one-student-at-a-time philosophy provide evidence that a goal of 90 percent graduation and 90 percent college enrollment for urban kids is attainable even if it is out of reach of the current traditional factory-school model.

In light of the current and future challenges facing the nation's youth, high school redesign and reform has become a rising issue of importance, capturing national attention. We must begin clearly focusing American high schools on the new purpose of preparing every student for full participation in a spectrum of postsecondary education opportunities, meaningful work, career advancement, and active citizenship.

Research indicates that high school redesign (specifically designs that emphasize rigor, relevance, and relationships) can reduce the achievement gap, increase graduation rates, improve access to postsecondary education, and ultimately help students succeed as economically secure adults.

Schools need to be challenged, but most proposals change form rather than substance. We don't need more hours of school every day and more days of school every year with schools as they are now. We don't need to train students to memorize information just to spit it back on tests. That produces nothing but the pretense of education, that students are being educated when they are not. This pretense of learning lies at the heart of student boredom and cynicism. Pretense, boredom, and cynicism are central elements in the destructive game (students spending their time and energy figuring out how to cut classes, learning to cheat, and wiggling out of doing schoolwork) that is the norm in American public high schools. We need schools that actively and meaningfully engage students in the process of their own learning. We need schools where the atmosphere is constructive, not destructive. There must be a connection between school learning and the world outside. Students deserve the chance to discover the joy and value of growing and learning as a lifelong activity.

The faults in the system of public education make me angry. We see an institution that appears to be satisfied educating kids at the lowest level of learning and growth, an institution that tends to stifle rather than encourage thinking and creativity in teachers as well as in students. The main function of this faulty system is teaching kids how to survive a gauntlet of classes, teachers, and administrators.

Schools are complex places. On one hand, they miss opportunities to truly educate students. On the other hand, most schools try to do the best they can, given the constraints under which they operate.

Teachers work very hard. Often they are not recognized for their successes. Many of the problems are beyond the scope of what the classroom teacher or the school administrator can solve. If we are to reform our schools, if we are serious about making public education work the way we want it to work, it is vital that we understand what really happens within a school.

So . . . How do we want it to work? Do we all want the same things? Obviously not. Besides assuming that everyone needs reading, writing, and math, there is not much agreement on what schools should do, let alone can do, as they are now structured.

People use the phrase *good education* all the time but never define what it means. Unless we define what we mean by good education, we have no clear and firm premise to work from in analyzing our schools and proposing changes. Very simply, I believe good education must provide a point of view from which what *is* can be seen clearly, what *was* can be seen as a living present, and what *will be* can be seen as filled with possibility. Now we have a starting point.

Next, we can ask ourselves, "What is the purpose of our public high schools?" It should be to educate young people to be thinking, reasoning, questioning, caring, aware citizens who acquire knowledge and information in the context of this purpose. Instead, it appears to be to jam as many isolated, often useless pieces of information as possible down students' throats so they can do well on tests, and above all, to give the appearance of having learned.

My proposals for change require high schools to be alive, exciting places where students *want* to come. Schools need a loving, inviting environment. Students must be treated as whole human beings who *want* to learn and grow and schools as places where students seek adult help and guidance in the process. Schools must be grounded in intellectual rigor. In high school, students should develop a lifelong love of learning, the desire to intelligently question authority and each other, and a genuine care for others. Teachers and administrators need to stop viewing kids as adversaries. Kids are younger intelligent human beings who are in school to be helped, not controlled and manipulated.

High schools should involve students in learning, be intellectually challenging, and be exciting, inviting, nurturing, and nonconfrontational. They should also promote self-directed and voluntary education and encourage personal growth and self-awareness.

The American system of secondary education is a reflection of American values and patterns just as the values of other countries are reflected in their educational systems. Without a radical change in basic societal values and practices, trying to adopt Japanese or European educational practices in the United States would be like trying to replace defective bricks with new ones without examining the foundation that supports the whole building.

The idea of an increased school day and year is a direct outgrowth of a Lego-model mentality. The catchphrase is "more instructional time." This clever carrot appeals to a common fallacy about teaching and learning: that learning is a static thing to be administered by teachers to students. Like stacking bricks one on top of the other to make a wall, the more time teachers have to present, the better.

This is sort of like the misconception people have about taking vitamins. Since one vitamin pill is supposed to be good for you, two must be that much better. We all know that is not necessarily true. Most definitely this analogy is not so when it comes to education: more of what we have now is not better, it is worse.

If the purpose of a public high school is to lift the tops off of students' heads and pour in facts and information, then the concept of instructional time may make some sense. But that is not what our secondary educational system should be about. I have said before that helping students learn information and facts is necessary, but is not the end in itself. The task is to help students develop their intellectual and personal potentials.

Americans have spent far more time discussing the idea of schools than the substance of education and structure of schools. Educators have been content to stick with the Lego model that evolved over the centuries. It's easier and people are used to it. It is as if we applied to the substance and structure of schools the adage, "If it ain't broke, don't fix it." Well, it is broke, and it does need fixing.

Let's take a good look at our high school students. Our students are capable of doing so much more learning and growing and, yes, "hard work," than they are generally asked to do in high schools. Hard work does not mean nightly busywork or six to seven hours a day of boring, tedious class in school. It means challenging students to think critically, to question intelligently, to be self-directed and self-disciplined, to do worthwhile research, to write more and better, and to take pride in themselves. Unfortunately, for most high school students, their learning amounts to listening to the teacher, memorizing material, and regurgitating it back on a test. There is little involvement, little expansion of intellectual horizons, and virtually no self-direction.

We keep saying that students need to be involved in the process of their own learning and growth. Why won't we let them? They need to see the value and purpose of what they are being asked to do. They need to be so excited about learning that it is not a chore but a satisfying challenge. In addition, students need to be involved in the life of their community and the world around them. Their formal educational experiences should mesh with the rest of their lives.

Given the degree to which the concepts of involvement, meaningful work, and self-direction are ignored in our high schools, one might think they are brand-new notions. But they are not. Progressive educators as far back as John Dewey, beginning at the end of the nineteenth century, and extending through Alfred Whitehead and Abraham Maslow and others in the early 1950s, have argued for a system of education that starts with the student, not the subject: a system of education that does not merely cram information down students' throats, but encourages students to grab for information, for knowledge, out of their own needs and interests. The basic idea is quite simple: if you start with the needs and feelings of young people as they see themselves, build on what they know and want, and then

introduce them to ideas and skills new to them, they are much more likely
to buy into what we adults think they should know.

Above all else, high school students need to be dealt with seriously as
young men and women moving into adulthood. They must not be infan-
tilized. That is, they must not be treated as if they need to be constantly
supervised and constantly reminded of what they are supposed to do. They
ought to test out things for themselves, learn by trial and error, and then
find out that it is okay to slip and fall now and then and that one can then
get up and carry on.

This does not mean that teachers or other adults should abandon kids
and let them run wild. Students, even high school seniors, want support
and assistance from adults. However, they want this from adults they trust,
adults they feel really care about them. Students do not want adults who
manipulate them and arrogantly try to impose their values and beliefs.
What kids need are adults who try to see the world through the eyes of
the kids, who offer guidance and suggestions after taking into account the
needs, feelings, and perceptions of the kids.

I am advocating an environment that challenges students intellectually
and also supports their need to grow personally, one being closely linked to
the other. For this to happen, students must be encouraged to be independent and self-directed learners during their growing-up years.

The challenge for teachers and students is to develop together ways of
helping students grow and learn. This is an ongoing process. The starting
point of the process, the framework in which the process takes place, must
be an articulated, understood assumption that high school–age young
people can develop intellectually and personally more fully than they are
generally encouraged or even permitted to do in the classrooms. Given
this, the possibilities for genuine student growth and learning are virtually
limitless.

The blunt truth is that the institution called a high school serves only part
of its target population very well, and then mainly as a conduit for society
to move that population on to college and good jobs. The high schools are
not doing what they should to help all young people to learn and grow.

There is very little chance of any significant reform within the secondary system as it remains. One of the main reasons is that the system is
entrenched. The high school format is the same as it was in the nineteenth
century, yet the world is a very different place today from what it was then.
Politics, sociology, economics, science, and technology have all joined together, causing the world to change tremendously in the last one hundred
years. And yet the high school remains the same. The thought of change
is frightening both for the general public that supports the system with its
taxes and those whose livelihood depend on it. Additionally, educators
are not trained to function in a we/we nonauthoritarian environment.

The system itself reinforces conformity and compliance, not creativity and questioning.

Why not put our fears aside and change the system? Improving our high schools could be a simple process. We can place the student at the center. Place the student first. All we need to do is to take the feelings of the kids seriously and let students in on what is happening and why. Give the students real-life meaningful work and responsibility. We can actively involve parents in the life of the school. Keeping class sizes small and varying the schedule of classes is an easy step. Teachers and administrators must be taught self-awareness and socioeconomic-political reality. Finally, allow more school-based management. Change becomes possible when individuals with different roles—students, teachers, administrators, and policymakers—interact around a shared concern for student learning. Most of the energy for change comes from those who are closest to the ground, students and teachers in the classrooms. Change must also grow from seeds already planted in different high schools, fed by a constant flow of human energy interacting across all levels of school organization.

We must look closely at the challenges. Added to the challenges of moving through adolescence in a time of great cultural stress are the increasing numbers of both low-income teenagers and recent arrivals to the United States, creating new and formidable tasks for the country and its educators.

In addition, so much attention has been paid to the needs of the college-bound student that many educators and citizens are concerned that the rest of the high school population has been forgotten. Far more money has been devoted to the education of the college-bound student both while the students are in high school and afterward.

What is needed are new pathways for entering into the economy and a breaking down of the barriers between school and work, permitting life-long learning to occur. A new approach to high school education is needed: more attention to basic skills (reading, writing, and math), social skills, and community involvement.

Educators are searching for ways to make large high schools feel smaller; smallness inside the larger whole, so to speak. Educators are hoping to transform the way the school *feels* to those who learn there.

The history of the U.S. high school has been the history of attempting to balance the twin goals of curriculum: richness and a sense of community. The curriculum must be one of rigor, breadth, diversity, and complexity joined with teacher subject specialization, delivering a content expertise that makes high standards inescapable.

Many educators, in their zeal to produce a world-class curriculum, overlooked the need to balance the curriculum with a sense of community, which would tie learners and teachers together in an interpersonal fabric of caring and concern for one another. We need high schools with both a rich and rigorous curriculum and a strong sense of community where teachers and students feel connected to one another in personal ways.

We also need to move away from strict departmentalization to interdisciplinary teams as a way to increase student success (the smaller high schools can use an advisor system where the teacher is responsible for the same students over a four-year period).

I have found that if a high school is effectively organized, achievement soars. A clear sense of purpose, leadership, professionalism, and high expectations for academic achievement were what really seemed to matter. Planning, team development, program development, and assessment will lead schools to achieve academic proficiency. Teacher empowerment and commitment to goals provide the energy for success. A commonly shared vision carries with it the energy and force to realize new outcomes. Let the vision become your guiding star.

Overall, today's administrators must buy into the new educational revolution. They must be able to change to enhance problem-solving capacity, empower groups to address pressing issues, and thrive to ever-higher levels of success.

Are we ready to accept the challenge? Let's explore reinventing the American high school.

First of all, let's set a goal of preparing *every* student for full participation in a spectrum of college opportunities, meaningful work, career advancement, and active citizenship.

All educators need to support students in the acquisition of rigorous core knowledge, skills, habits, and attitudes needed for success in postsecondary education and the highly skilled workplace. We need to engage students in specific career-related learning experiences that equip them to make well-informed decisions about further education and training and employment opportunities. We also must prepare students who may choose to enter the workforce directly after high school with a level of skill and knowledge in a particular career area that will be valued in the marketplace.

In light of the current and future challenges facing our youth, I believe we need a new working model for high schools. The globalization of business and industry requires workers to acquire core knowledge and skills that can be applied, and quickly upgraded and adapted, in a wide and rapidly changing work setting.

Any observer can clearly see serious problems emerging in the educational outcomes of young Americans: high dropout rates, inadequate communications, insufficient math and science skills, high postsecondary remediation rates, and large achievement gaps caused by race and income. These performance indicators suggest a major problem with the American educational system and, specifically, the goals and culture of today's American high school.

Far too many young people leave high school before earning diplomas. These students are not engaged in the high school experience and don't consider the curriculum relevant, and teachers find that the academic programs too often fail to help students who have not mastered academic content to catch up. On the other hand, far too many students earn high school diplomas without possessing the knowledge and skills necessary for success in college or the workplace.

The United States is beset by three education gaps. The first gap is the domestic achievement gap, the disparity in learning among American students, which is correlated to racial and economic status. The second gap is an international achievement gap between American students and young people from other nations who are more highly educated and, in many cases, able to carry out skilled work for relatively low wages compared to what skilled American workers command in the workplace. Even more disturbing are aspects of American culture that are devaluing hard work, personal achievement, exerting effort toward reaching future goals, and other aspects of strong character. These factors are contributing to an overall lack of focus and purpose among American youth that has recently been termed the ambition gap.

In a speech before the nation's governors, and business and educational leaders in February 2005, Microsoft Corporation founder Bill Gates made a provocative statement about American high schools: "American high schools are obsolete. By obsolete, I mean that our high schools, even when they are working exactly as designed, cannot teach our kids what they need to know today. Training the workforce of tomorrow with high schools of today is like trying to teach kids about today's computers on a 50-year-old mainframe. It is the wrong tool for the times." This is a hard-hitting statement, but it deserves serious consideration. Is the American high school obsolete?

During the twentieth century, education decisionmakers worked hard to design schools that were aligned to their aspirations for a healthy society where individuals from different social classes were satisfied with their standing and were doing work that was appropriate to their abilities and interests. Vocational programs were designed for students who had strong aptitudes for technology, installation, and repair of machinery and entry into the skilled trades. College preparatory programs were designed for the management cadre that would direct the production of the workforce, and for the preparation of other professionals such as accountants, lawyers, physicians, political leaders, and the clergy. For other students, a general education was taught, which included reading, writing, some math, and "life adjustment" courses that were enough to prepare any industrious young person to enter the middle class.

The American high school we know today harkens back to the ideal of the large comprehensive high school endorsed in 1959 by James Conant in the definitive report of its day, "The American High School." In this landmark report, which codified much thinking around high schools, Conant claimed that only 15 percent of high school students had the mental ability to take rigorous courses in mathematics, science, and foreign languages.

At the time Conant wrote, midway through the twentieth century, many reformers and educators thought the recommendations for the comprehensive American high school were well grounded, but as we look back, biases and stereotypes were lurking just beneath the surface of assumptions about the purpose of high schools. Furthermore, educational leaders misjudged how quickly the U.S. economy would change in the latter part of the century and how high-level skills would become needed across a wider spectrum of the workforce.

Given the realities of the twenty-first century global economy and the continuing demands for increased knowledge and skills it is placing on the American workforce, the model of high school education the United States has known for the past fifty years is now obsolete. It was designed for a different era and a set of core beliefs that are no longer valid in modern society.

Many of the twentieth-century assumptions about the comprehensive high school, designed for tracking and sorting, prevailed until dismay with educational outcomes was given voice by the National Commission on Excellence in Education through the *A Nation at Risk* report in 1983.

Since that time, federal and state policy design has been based to a greater and greater degree upon the premise that all students need a core set of academic skills and competencies that can help them become lifelong learners and adaptable knowledge workers. Specifically, school reform efforts at the national and state levels focused on identifying specific education standards, creating assessment linked to those standards, and implementing accountability systems that would focus the attention of teachers, administrators, and students on developing the knowledge and skills called for in those standards.

This movement of standards-based reform was catalyzed through a series of events, reports, and legislation during the 1990s. It was given further momentum through the No Child Left Behind Act of 2001, which created a national framework for how states would measure, report, and hold schools accountable for their performance against these standards. While NCLB does not focus extensively on high schools, it does reinforce and promote a level of academic rigor at this level, although most of the actual state assessments are pegged at eighth- and ninth-grade–level reading and mathematics. Even prior to NCLB, many states began to undertake efforts to ensure that all students reach minimum levels of academic proficiency by the time they graduate by imposing new requirements, such as end-of-course exams, high-stakes exams required for graduation, and increases in coursework requirements for high school graduation.

In light of the current and future challenges facing our youth I believe a new working model for the American high school is long overdue. The new model cannot be created just to fix problems of the past. It must be created with the future in mind and be designed around the needs of today and tomorrow's students.

I would suggest the following recommendations as a guide to the reinvention of the American high school.

ESTABLISH A CLEAR SYSTEM GOAL OF CAREER AND COLLEGE READINESS FOR ALL STUDENTS

All students need a strong arsenal of reading, comprehension, reasoning, problem-solving, and personal skills to be ready for the world of meaningful postsecondary education and training as well as entry to the high-skilled workplace. The importance of a broad and rigorous preparation for today's students cannot be overstated. Students are not simply preparing for education and training related to today's jobs. They must be prepared to continuously learn and innovate to stay competitive in a highly connected international marketplace and to help create new types of jobs that do not yet exist.

It makes sense to establish an objective of having all students graduate from high school fully ready to participate in postsecondary education, and of significantly increasing the number of students who not only enter college but persist in college and succeed in earning degrees and/or skill certificates. All students will need to make their own choices about if, when, and how they participate in postsecondary education, but young adults need to be prepared to engage in some type of postsecondary courses and training to have viable career options.

We need to shift from the sorting-and-selecting "multiplex" approach for academic classes that still prevails in most high schools. To make this work, programs will need to be explicitly directed to align their instructional programs with these expectations in mind, giving students extra help and support on an as-needed basis to keep them on grade level as they move toward graduation.

We also need to ensure smooth transitions between eighth and ninth grade in order to target special help for incoming ninth graders who are behind grade level, and to whenever possible create summer bridge programs to jump-start the high school years. In a related manner, as schools eliminate low-level courses from the high school curriculum, they will need to create extra help, tutoring, and new versions of courses that teach to the same academic standards but over an extended instructional period or in an applied setting.

A renewed focus also must be placed on the transition of students from high school into further education and career opportunities. Students should be given the opportunity while in high school to take postsecondary entrance and skill certification exams. Postsecondary education credits earned while in high school need to be accepted by the colleges and universities.

CREATE A POSITIVE SCHOOL CULTURE THAT STRESSES PERSONALIZATION IN PLANNING AND DECISION MAKING

Students entering high school today were born around 1995. When we think about the pace of the changes in information technologies, wireless communications, and global interconnectedness that have occurred since their birth, it is clear that today's high school students have vastly different and more complex life experiences than the young people of the 1930s, 1940s, and 1950s, for whom the prevailing high school model was designed. Students with access to information technology and wireless communication can, in their out-of-school life, access information and learning on an anytime, anywhere basis. They can interact with commercial, learning, and gaming resources in ways that are highly individualized and customized to their particular interests and tastes. Yet our industrial model of education continues to treat students as parts of a mechanistic system, expecting them to fit into the system rather than investing in them as uniquely gifted individuals.

At a minimum, every student should be led through a process of academic and career awareness, exploration, and planning. This should include learning about the economy and career options; self-assessment for areas of interest; and knowledge and understanding of local, state, and national educational, occupational, and labor-market opportunities, needs, and trends. These skills are necessary in order to make informed educational choices, which lead to more education and career options. An individualized plan that leads to graduation and beyond that is updated often as students' interests solidify is a start.

As we are creating a new culture that spurs every student on to his or her highest individual potential, the school needs to encourage students to reach for challenging personal goals and see themselves rising to management and leadership roles within their chosen professions. At the same time we must make sure the system does not prescribe one-size-fits-all solutions (e.g., going to a four-year college) for each and every student, but guides and supports students and their parents or guardians in the decision-making process. In the reinvented American high school, students will be given the structured opportunity to identify their evolving personal interests and interactively connect those interests to their future.

CREATE A POSITIVE SCHOOL CULTURE THAT STRESSES PERSONALIZATION IN RELATIONSHIPS

During the second half of the twentieth century, as traditional social bonds in communities were weakening, high schools themselves were getting bigger, due in part to the recommendations of Conant's "The American High School." For those adolescents who already have weak family and community connections, these enormous schools become places of anonymity, encourage them to withdraw further into the shadows, and make them more vulnerable to the allure of negative peer reinforcements such as drugs, alcohol, sex, and crime.

A fair, consistent, and challenging code of discipline is an absolute prerequisite to establishing a positive school culture, but discipline is not enough in and of itself. Positive relationships built on the foundation of respect, citizenship, and order are the deeper goal for the school culture. Schools remain one of the best opportunities for connecting youth and adults in positive ways, giving students the sense that they are valued and cared for, and reinforcing the message that whether they succeed or fail actually matters to someone.

During the past ten years, a strong reform movement has developed, with the goal of transforming large impersonal high schools into places that feel smaller, safer, and more personal to the student. Small high schools of about four hundred or fewer students have been founded to maximize relationships and connectedness. Daily advisory periods are another strategy that creates a structured environment to connect an adult with a small group of students for personal interaction and activities like character education, career development, and social and study skills.

Creating a culture that stresses relationships will require significant change, particularly among the many teachers who believe their job is to only teach subject matter. High schools should establish the goal of helping every student become involved, whether it be through an advisory period, a smaller learning community, or a cocurricular, interest-based activity that strengthens positive relationships and encourages the student's sense of confidence and belonging in school. In addition we need to encourage community leaders to become engaged in these educational activities to provide students with additional opportunities for positive adult relationships.

DRAMATICALLY IMPROVE HOW
ACADEMIC CONTENT IS TAUGHT

Higher levels of knowledge and skills in academic content are absolutely necessary for our high school students, but school leaders will make a serious miscalculation if they just add more challenging courses without changing the way courses are taught.

Today, I have found that many students who take a full complement of college preparatory classes in high school still need college-level remedial classes. Reading and mathematics performance by seventeen-year-old students taking the National Assessment of Education Progress has remained absolutely flat. I conclude that the achievement problem is not just one of taking low-level courses, it is also related to unfocused curriculum and weak instructional methods that are not reaching all students.

Teachers and researchers must work together to identify strategies that show promise for helping all students attain proficiency in high-level courses. Let's keep expectations constant, but vary time and teaching style.

In the new American high school, the entire school must own the mission of academic proficiency, and teachers should be required to collaborate across the disciplines to help students reach these proficiencies.

CREATE INCENTIVES FOR STUDENTS TO PURSUE THE
CORE CURRICULUM THROUGH INTEREST-BASED CONTENT

Many students are bored and disengaged with today's schools. In their personal lives they often pursue various forms of on-demand learning related to hobbies and interests. However, during the school day, the knowledge to which they are exposed is usually disembodied from its real-world context. They learn science facts and theories, but do not understand the work of chemists or biotechnologists. Students are asked to improve their writing structure and grammar, but do not see how effective writing is employed in developing persuasive business proposals, creating research, writing articles or books, or simply engaging in day-to-day workplace communications. They don't see the relevance of the school curriculum to their current or future lives.

Relevance is an essential motivator for individual effort for both youth and adults. Connecting rigorous academic expectations with the relevance of an interest-based curriculum, often related to a career theme, can help connect students to learning in powerful ways. Interest-based areas can be organized around various broad themes, such as the fine arts, or more specific themes like biotechnology, preengineering, hospitality, or finance.

I suggest that robust interest-based programs contain the following essential elements: require or strongly encourage a rigorous career and college readiness academic program for all students; provide every student with sophisticated career exploration and career development services; encourage qualified students to take advanced placement and dual enrollment coursework in upper grades; emphasize the use of challenging projects that integrate learning and leadership development; and encourage internships and work-based learning to help students grow in maturity, gain exposure to the adult world of work, and develop strong social skills.

SUPPORT HIGH-QUALITY TEACHING IN ALL CONTENT AREAS

NCLB creates mechanisms for ensuring that every teacher in the academic core subjects is highly qualified, meaning the teacher holds a bachelor's degree or higher, grasps content at a deep level, and can teach that content effectively. There is concern, however, that while the intent of the highly qualified teacher requirement is sound, the compromises made during the passage of NCLB allowed most current teachers to be considered highly qualified simply by counting their years of experience and possession of a teaching certificate, rather than objectively measuring content and teaching expertise. Standards for knowledge measuring content-teaching expertise need to be effectively applied to veteran teachers as well as new teachers.

OFFER FLEXIBLE LEARNING OPPORTUNITIES TO ENCOURAGE REENTRY AND COMPETITION

True quality high school reform must include effective strategies to reengage and reconnect young people who are in danger of failing or who have failed to complete high school. These young people have failed according to the current high school system. To reform high school without a strategy to reengage these young people who have already dropped out would be to abandon them, too, and accept the social costs associated with bleak futures marked by reduced earning potential, poverty, crime, drug abuse, and early pregnancy.

Developing flexible education programs requires that education leaders broaden their responsibility from responsibility for students who are enrolled to responsibility for *all* youth in the community, in addition to responsibility for dependable and equitable sources of funding for staff, curriculum, technology, facilities, and professional development. All students, including young people who have dropped out of school, need a continuum of flexible interest-based learning opportunities that utilize effective teaching methodologies and are responsive to their varied needs and life circumstances. Dropout recovery efforts should not only focus on helping dropouts to return to high school, but also on connecting them to a range of options and activities, including dual high school and college credit, leadership development opportunities, and work-readiness credentials that lead to high school diplomas and employment opportunities.

Recovering those young people who fail to graduate high school every year also requires educational leaders and policymakers to shift their thinking about alternative schools and education. High school reform efforts should embrace the notion that all secondary educational programs, whether traditional or alternative, belong to one educational system that meets a range of student needs and offers a continuum of learning opportunities that helps secondary students to quickly and efficiently prepare to succeed in postsecondary education and the workforce.

Particularly for students who have dropped out, interest-based career courses, those that have a clear employment connection, may be the most likely to motivate the student to reengage in education. Returning dropouts should be encouraged to use career-based classes, credit-recovery programs, technology supports that address specific academic needs, and flexible schedules of evening, morning, and weekend programs.

Many students who reengage in school will do so under real-life circumstances that prevent them from transitioning back to high school. Moreover, it does not make sense to expect students who are experiencing academic success in alternative environments to return to the traditional high school setting, where they initially became disconnected and lost interest. It makes more sense to create multiple points of access for students to reengage in alternative programs that can meet the students' real-life needs while helping them to earn their high school diplomas and credentials that employers value.

CREATE SYSTEM INCENTIVES AND SUPPORTS

Policymakers at the federal, state, and local levels should see academic and interest-based courses as complements of one another and create incentives that support the building of rich, interest-based programs around a core of rigorous academic expectations.

We also need to create stronger and richer accountability for high school performance, create assessments of career and college readiness, and support local innovations in curriculum, instructional delivery, and professional development that are essential for improved student achievement.

MOVE BEYOND "SEAT TIME" AND
NARROWLY DEFINED KNOWLEDGE AND SKILLS

U.S. high schools operate on a well-established set of expectations for size, time of day and seasons of the year that programs and classes are offered, how instructional material is delivered, and what constitutes success in terms of the students' knowledge and skills. If our education system adopts the new goal of getting every student ready for careers and college and changes the way teachers teach, it will create a degree of conflict with those accepted norms of how schools currently operate and the policies that sustain this environment. I suggest that we focus on which knowledge and skills are measured, how students are asked to determine their knowledge and skills, and how school is offered for all young people, particularly for the many students who are currently disengaged and leaving or have already left the traditional high school.

In contrast to measuring real student learning, much of the current discussion around high school reform focuses on increasing course-taking requirements. Time-bound course taking is a crude proxy for knowing whether a student is gaining knowledge and skills. Furthermore, placing the emphasis on imparting academic knowledge and skills only through narrowly defined courses could actually impede innovations in the way content can be accessed by students.

Ultimately, a true standards-based approach to education requires moving away from the time-based Carnegie unit approach that measures inputs to one that measures outputs, what the student has learned and can do. Until reliable assessments of knowledge and skills are in place, it will be difficult to let go of the seat-time approach. A first step toward the new vision is to continue using existing assessments for accountability and exit requirements while also developing and implementing performance-based demonstrations of skills and knowledge that can give a richer picture of the students' skills.

School reform advocates generally agree that preparation for further education and the workforce requires more than traditional core academic skills like reading and mathematics. These skills are essential, but they are not sufficient in and of themselves. Often, however, accountability systems are largely focused only on these narrowly defined and narrowly assessed academic skills. Admittedly, the soft skills of reasoning, problem solving, teamwork, leadership, and social maturity are difficult to quantify. Still, the adage of "what gets measured gets taught" is very real, so there must be a clear incentive for schools to also focus on the development of students' soft skills and aptitudes.

Designing American high schools around the needs of students in the present and the future requires honesty, courage, and a willingness to change familiar structures and practices in the best interests of our young people. It does not mean abandoning all current practices or resources. It means identifying those practices that are working and restructuring the policy and support systems to make those options accessible to each student. It will require a mix of approaches, jettisoning negative culture and outdated practices, thoughtfully realizing and adjusting current resources, and making new investments to build faculty and program capacities. Real change, made for the right reasons and toward the right mission, will yield dramatically better results and a more hopeful future for America's young people and for our national economic and cultural well-being.

How are we able to use rigor, relevance, and relationships to improve student achievement and reform our high schools? Let's steal some best practices from high schools making good progress in raising student achievement and thus reforming their schools.

A common thread among these schools is that all teach challenging academic studies and quality career and technical studies. Four major themes emerged from the efforts of these schools.

First is teaching all students a rigorous academic core, which includes credits in college-prep/honors English; math credits, including algebra 1 and 2, geometry, and trigonometry; and higher science credits as well as social studies credits at the college-prep level for at least three years.

An English/language arts curriculum should emphasize reading and writing across the curriculum, which helps deepen students' use of language and vocabulary as well as comprehension, analysis, writing, and speaking. Heritage Hills High School in Indiana, Galax High School in Virginia, and Carolina High School and Academy in South Carolina are examples of schools excelling in this area.

When it comes to improving mathematics, all teachers at South Cobb High School in Georgia incorporate problem-solving activities into the daily curriculum. Students at Buford High School in Georgia write about mathematics problems and orally defend their solutions.

Science curriculum is taught in engaging ways that motivate students to learn. Schools are emphasizing reading and mathematics in science classes, linking science to real life, getting students to write and talk about their laboratory findings, and showing how science forms the basis for many careers and technical fields. Minuteman Regional High School in Massachusetts requires students to complete a science-based senior project that demonstrates what they have learned in four years at the school. Barnwell High School in South Carolina places a major emphasis on project-based learning in science classes.

The second theme is making learning relevant and meaningful to students. These schools offer high-quality career and technical courses designed to prepare students for broad career fields and postsecondary studies. Sussex Technical High School in Delaware and Columbia County Career and Technical Center in Ohio integrate academic and technical/employability competencies in chosen career fields.

Several schools use worksite learning as a way to advance school-based academic and technical learning. Veteran workers take students under their wings, showing them how to do the work and how to develop the workplace habits and customer relations skills that are so vital to success in business and industry. York County School of Technology in Pennsylvania and Queen Anne's County High School in Maryland closely monitor students to ensure that academic learning is connected to on-the-job learning. A strong guidance system is also in place, helping students to make wise choices about further education and a career. Mentors from the community also assist.

Providing support and personal relationships makes up the third theme. These schools are not just spouting rhetoric when they say they truly believe every student deserves to learn at a high level. More teachers in more classrooms at these schools are willing to go the extra mile in providing extra help. Wheeler High School in Indiana and Springfield High School in Arkansas have made real gains in achievement with students who participate in the after-school programs.

Improving the transition from middle grades to high school is another way to guarantee success. If students have weak academic skills when they enter ninth grade, they are more apt to lose interest in school and even drop out before graduating. High schools are taking the initiative to identify and provide special catch-up courses for incoming freshmen who are unprepared for challenging high school classes. James Madison High School in Texas conducts a summer bridge program for students from the feeder middle-grade schools who risk failing in the first year of high school.

Finally, these schools make their senior years count. Schools do students a favor when they forbid slacking off in the twelfth grade. A rigorous senior year ensures that graduates are ready for the demands of postsecondary education and a career.

The fourth theme is providing leadership and faculty support for continued improvement. Successful school leaders do not simply ask teachers to do a better job in meeting the school's goals and objectives, they make it possible for all teachers to learn how to teach more effectively. Good schools focus on continuous improvement. Destrehan High School in Louisiana is organized so teachers will be able to participate fully in making decisions about curriculum and instruction.

The examples in this chapter are intended to motivate school and district leaders to examine where they are and where they want to be in preparing high school students for future careers. I would recommend that schools consider the following actions: create a common understanding among teachers and administration about what students need to learn, what constitutes good

teaching, and what kinds of assessments and student work meet standards at
the level necessary for students to continue their education; provide generous assistance to help incoming and current students complete challenging
programs of study; and link with postsecondary institutions and employers
to ensure that students are taking the right academic and career and technical courses throughout high school and are receiving the best experiences to
ensure success after graduation. Districts can assist by raising curriculum and
instructional standards and conducting frequent audits to determine if teachers' assessments are helping students meet the standards necessary for success
in postsecondary studies and in the job market and by providing professional
development to help teachers inject research-based strategies into their instruction to develop students as independent learners.

We can even take this one step further and suggest the states hold all
schools accountable for making progress in preparing students to pursue
postsecondary studies and collect, analyze, and disseminate data designed
to assist schools in their quest for higher achievement.

A frank dialogue between educational professionals is one of the best
ways to gain insights about practices that could work at your own school.
Remember, none of the schools mentioned earlier are perfect, but all of
them are very good and getting better as they strive to raise standards,
improve teacher instruction and assessments, use best practices, and teach
students how to become independent learners.

The state of Hawaii has taken this step. Hawaii's vision of a high school
graduate is that each student will realize his or her individual goals and objectives; possess the attitudes, knowledge, and skills necessary to contribute
positively; compete in a global society; exercise the rights and responsibilities of citizenship; and pursue postsecondary education and/or career options without need for remediation.

Let me share with you what one Hawaiian high school accomplished with
its reform initiatives. Leina High is a sprawling school of low bungalows in a
semirural corner of Oahu. The neighboring community of Leina is one of the
few remaining areas in Oahu with a large percentage of Native Hawaiians. It
is also one of the most economically depressed areas in the state.

Leina High's character is shaped by that of the neighboring community.
Half the students are Native Hawaiian and many of the remainder are
Samoan and Filipino immigrants. Most qualify for free or reduced lunch
programs. Some live in homeless encampments on nearby beaches. Twice
as many are performing below grade level as in the national norm. Of those
able to graduate, the majority seek work, join the military, or study part
time at a nearby community college.

To better meet the challenges the school faces, Leina administrators have
launched an aggressive reform campaign. At the center of the reform plan
is a school-to-work plan to better prepare students for success in Hawaii's

competitive economy. As part of the planned reform, students are encouraged to select a career pathway, such as arts and communication, business and management, health services, human services, or natural resources, and then take a number of selected courses in that particular pathway while also participating in extracurricular activities such as visits to local workplaces.

The school has broken out of the traditional classroom disciplines. Teachers are designing projects across disciplines. They are also breaking down traditional teacher-student roles. Students are working independently, pursuing areas of their own interest.

Flexible scheduling was introduced at Leina High. Mondays, Tuesdays, and Fridays were organized according to a traditional six-period high school program. Wednesdays and Thursdays were based on two-hour classes to allow for students carrying out independent projects. Teacher initiative and involvement rounded out the reform. Teachers are devoting untold hours and boundless energy to reshaping students' attitudes and providing them with skills to help better compete in the job market.

In general, the key to success for restructuring high schools is a continuous improvement model in which the most current data available will drive all decision making in the implementation and delivery of instruction and other program segments. The secondary team (core teachers, administration, and support staff) will become a learning community in which data will regularly be reviewed to make decisions regarding instruction and improvement of program delivery. Decision making will be collaborative. All elements of the program should be scrutinized for analysis. Other program elements and/or strategies may be designed and implemented to resolve questions raised by current data (proficiency; student performance; parent, student, and staff surveys; staff development; and process, including discipline policies).

The restructuring of the high schools should take into account and consideration the affective as well as the cognitive needs of all students. It is the combination of synergy and the convergence of the affective and cognitive needs that actively motivates and engages students in the educational process. The dynamics are such that if input includes a variety of elements from both domains, the program will be more compelling and the level of student engagement will be much improved. Successful educational programming will be systematic and deeply embedded in the educational organization. Each element put in place will be like a piece of a jigsaw puzzle. Each piece contributes to the whole, but by itself will have limited value. Remember, academic talent alone does not guarantee achievement. However, through recognition of the talent the student may be encouraged to achieve beyond mediocrity.

Therefore, the framework for program development recognizes both the affective (relationships, recognition, relevance, and family/community support) and cognitive (general ability, aptitude, and interests) development of students in connection to the level and sophistication of curricular delivery.

It has been suggested that over 90 percent of instruction in our high schools is memorization and understanding, the two lowest levels of instruction. We must move to the higher levels of instruction (application, analysis, synthesis, and evaluation) to better engage students in the educational process. By moving to higher levels all students are cognitively challenged, particularly those who have a creative interest. To create is to inject a piece of oneself into the process, and for many students this is highly motivating. I firmly believe that when the higher cognitive levels of instruction are implemented, with recognition for productive thinking, respectful dialogue, open-ended divergent questioning, and relevant topics, students will become engaged in the educational process. The greater the convergence between cognitive instruction, ability, aptitude, and interest and affective interests and needs, the greater the impact on our nation's youth.

The following are suggestions for affective and cognitive programming within your high school restructuring plan.

AFFECTIVE PROGRAMMING

Be aware of listening posts: satisfaction surveys (students and parents), compliance surveys (implementation of programs), staff surveys, circle sharing (small groups to share feelings regarding topics presented by staff), and parent advisory committees. Conduct student/parent orientation prior to the opening of school in the fall and first-day-of-school activities to create a welcoming atmosphere.

Also include an advisor/advisee program, student ambassador program, honor society, student of the week, attendance awards, student arts and literary publications (including prose, poetry, drawings, paintings, and photography), school yearbooks, senior retreat, and student council.

In addition, keep in mind that discipline is the key to academic success and good classroom management brings this about. Student behavior needs to be appropriate to ensure an optimal learning environment. A dean of students/guidance counselor will provide support, track student progress toward graduation, and help students prepare for postsecondary education or the world of work.

COGNITIVE PROGRAMMING

It is important to have basic productivity skills in order to improve the possibility of securing or maintaining employment and improve academic success. Keyboarding, formatting a word processing document, designing a spreadsheet, and developing a PowerPoint are necessary skills to have. They are no longer an option in today's world of work, but are required for work readiness whether workers are skilled, semiskilled, or nonskilled. Direct instruction with guided practice is necessary for math achievement, as the development of a strong sustained silent reading program is for language arts.

In addition, include extracurricular academic or athletic programs, advanced placement programs, student support classes, and if the school program warrants, an exchange program with cultural experiences. (An American Indian charter school in Minneapolis developed a three-day experience at a traditional Indian village at the Leech Lake Indian Reservation, where students stayed in a traditional log house and learned traditional skills used by their ancestors.)

Finally, professional development will be key to the success of any restructuring effort. Staff should form collaborative learning communities and utilize data to drive decision making in order to design and develop programs and improve instructional delivery. Teachers should also be encouraged to develop professional learning plans to target skills they wish to develop further. Emphasis will be on improving instructional practice through improved classroom management and on providing more opportunities for students to experience higher-level thinking and use problem-solving skills.

How do we meet the challenges facing high school reform today? High school reform has moved to the top of the educational policy agenda, commanding the attention of the federal government, governors, urban school superintendents, philanthropists, and the general public. All are alarmed by stubbornly high dropout rates, by the low academic achievement of many high school students, and by the large numbers of high school graduates who are required to take remedial classes in college. These trends disproportionately affect urban and certain rural areas and minority groups and disadvantaged young people, especially those who are African American, Hispanic, and American Indian who attend urban schools and the rural schools of the South and Southwest.

Structural changes to improve personalization and instructional improvement are the twin pillars of high school reform. Small learning communities and faculty advisory systems can increase students' feelings of connectedness to their teachers and schools.

Nevertheless, challenges exist. Creating a personalized and orderly learning environment is a challenge. A positive school climate, where students and adults know each other well and where adults express concern for students' well-being, intellectual growth, and academic success, is a key motivational element in the learning process for adolescents.

Challenge two is assisting students who enter high school with poor academic skills. You can tackle this challenge head-on through interconnected changes in the scheduling and curricula, including catch-up courses.

Challenge three is improving instructional content and practice. Teachers in schools serving disadvantaged populations are often less experienced and less knowledgeable about subjects they teach than teachers in more affluent communities. How to improve the content and delivery of what is taught should be tied to professional development. Student achievement may be enhanced by professional development activities that involve teachers working together to align curricula and standards and discuss ways of making classroom activities more engaging.

Preparing students for the world beyond high school is our fourth challenge. All students need special assistance in preparing for postsecondary education and for better-paying jobs.

The final challenge that I see associated with reforming high schools is stimulating change: introducing change into high schools and making it stick. Change demands an investment of personal resources, including a hard look at what is already in place. Avoid jumping from one reform to the next. Stay the course until initiatives have been put in place long enough to receive a fair test. In addition, it is important to have high ambitions but also reasonable expectations about the impact that reforms can produce.

In summary, the academic problems that economically disadvantaged students face in high school generally begin long before ninth grade. Many such students enter high school without the basic skills in reading and mathematics that will enable them to succeed in more demanding courses. Unable to do well, they are all too likely to stop trying, to cut classes, and, ultimately, to drop out entirely.

Teachers are often less experienced and may avoid giving challenging assignments. Instead, their lessons may entail repeated drill in basic skills, further alienating students from the learning process.

These problems are exacerbated in the large, impersonal, and sometimes unsafe environments of many comprehensive urban high schools. Students and teachers do not get to know each other or to develop bonds of caring and trust. Guidance counselors, called on to intervene with students who are chronically absent or who present behavior problems, are frequently too overburdened to give all students the guidance they need to select the right courses for college admission or even for high school graduation. Finally, in these large schools, there may be no one who can help students understand the connection between what they are studying and their lives after high school. Students who see their classes as both extremely difficult and irrelevant to their futures have little reason to remain in school. Also, how students fare in ninth grade and whether they are promoted on time to tenth grade are good prognosticators of whether students will succeed in the rest of their high school courses.

We must focus on creating environments that are conductive to learning, utilizing catch-up skills programs, improving instructional content and delivery, preparing students for postsecondary education and employment, and investing in personnel resources and time needed to bring about changes that are ambitious yet achievable.

In order to choose the course of action that is most appropriate, ask yourself a series of questions: In tackling what is to be done, are you starting from scratch? If some reforms are already in place, are you satisfied with how they are operating? Do you have the personnel to design and implement a new reform? Even if you have the capacity to change, do you have the time? Planning time is a key consideration in instituting reform. You also need time for the reform to register effects. It is important to understand that the impacts of reform efforts are seldom large and dramatic.

Reform initiatives should not be quickly replaced; they should be improved. Program developers need to identify weaknesses both in concept and in practice and move to strengthen them quickly. School personnel need to work toward more effective and consistent implementation. Over time, one can hope to see better and better outcomes, not through huge leaps forward, but as the cumulative effort of many small steps in the right direction. High school reform must be a building block of an overall effort to improve the nation's schools.

In all these recommendations about redesigning the American high school, these points must be reemphasized. First, it will be a tragic miscalculation to pit academic course taking against access to rigorous career-oriented and interest-based programs. Students need to be taught in a way that is rigorous, relevant to their areas of personal interest and career aspirations, and that leads to a supportive environment of relationships.

Second, none of the proposed redesign functions will work unless there is a sense of shared accountability at the school level for raising the performance of every student. Without external accountability and a notion of what is promising and what works, there will not be enough impetus to overcome traditional teaching methods and organizational isolation.

Third, creating a positive high school environment that emphasizes rigor, relevance, and relationships requires a talented and committed leadership team.

We need a radical departure from the present system. The premise of a new system should be to provide a framework and mechanism for all young people to continue learning in every way possible and to test out that learning in the world around them in order to discover paths along which they want to take their lives. We as educators need to focus on the environment in which young people are invited to grow and learn, are involved in the process of their own learning, are excited about it, are intellectually challenged, and are given every opportunity to become self-directed learners. The focus should be on adults nurturing the youth.

Shaping the future of American high schools centers on a new mission, preparing every young person for meaningful work, lifelong learning and career advancement, and active citizenship in our rapidly changing global community.

6

School Choice

The purpose of life is to love it, to taste experience to the utmost, to reach
out eagerly and without fear for newer and richer experiences.

—Eleanor Roosevelt

Touted as an unsinkable ship of social progress for more than a century,
public schooling is leaking badly. Achievement is stagnant or declining,
public opinion is low, and community conflict over what is taught seems to
be ever-increasing. Some schools, especially in the inner city, have already
slid beneath the waves, extinguishing the educational hopes and dreams
of countless children. Literally thousands of would-be reformers have suggested patches here and there, but the water just keeps flooding in.

Perhaps the most detailed current educational reform measure is parental
school choice. Under school choice programs, geographic restrictions are
eliminated and parents are allowed to choose their child's school.

Advocates of choice programs argue that expanding parents' choice of
schools will improve public education by introducing competition into the
educational system. Because parents could choose the best public or private
schools for their children, less effective schools would be forced to improve
their quality to compete for students and remain open.

Opponents argue that school choice would harm public schools because
parents would choose schools that matched their children's ethnic or social-
class characteristics. Critics contend such segregation would reverse the
progress achieved by years of integration of students of all backgrounds.

If the education of the next generation is not to be completely forsaken,
we need to cast aside our assumptions about how schools should be run

and consider not only major overhauls to the current system but entirely different approaches as well.

Realistically, we first have to understand people's educational needs before we can determine which sorts of school systems most effectively serve those needs. Public opinion around the world shows that there is a fundamental kernel of agreement among parents on the importance of basic academic subjects. People expect that, as a minimum, their children will have mastered reading, writing, and elementary math by the time they are out of high school. There is an equally strong emphasis on career preparation, since parents from Milwaukee to Munich consider landing a good job to be one of the main purposes of education.

Beyond these basics, priorities diverge wildly. Whenever a state-run school system adopts one set of priorities at the expense of all others, conflict inevitably ensues. Consider the battles over religion in the classroom that have plagued the United States for over a hundred years and the rest of the world for centuries before that.

Clearly we need a system that can cater to differences between families, but what about people without school-aged children? To the extent that the general public subsidizes education by whatever means, it can rightly ask that its needs be met as well. Fortunately, parents and nonparents agree that basic academics and career preparation are the keys. Most people also consider any contribution that schooling can make to the harmony of social relations and the productivity of economic relations desirable. Finally, citizens expect to get their money's worth from the schools. If costs increase and taxes are raised, student achievement should go up as well.

Educational reformers have suggested a whole range of strategies for improving our schools, from new curricula and tougher standards to charter schools, vouchers, and even complete privatization.

We need to know what has worked and what has not and why. What history shows us is that the problems of high spending, lack of successful innovation, unresponsiveness to the needs of families, and social strife over what is taught are mainly caused by the way public schools are run, not by the people who staff them or the particular standards or curricula they adopt.

It appears to be the absence of competition between schools that stifles innovation and inflates prices, the lack of potential profit that makes applied educational research and development a waste of money and time, and the lack of parental freedom of choice that sets family against family in a bitter fight for ideological control of the schools. Overall, we can have the educational outcomes we want (higher academic achievement, effective innovation, social harmony, responsive teachers, reasonable costs, etc.) if we allow school choice. It is hoped that school choices will help all citizens to assess the merits of the educational system and offer parents the best choice for the future of their children and communities.

Choice abounds in America. It is the cornerstone of our nation. Education is no different. Today's parents face an abundance of choices when deciding where and how to educate their children. This array of options can be both a blessing and a curse.

Choice is growing in popularity. Parents consider options for their children that range from publicly funded private schools to homeschooling, from profit-making schools to charter and magnet schools. All possibilities have their strengths. All deserve consideration if America is serious about renewing its troubled educational system.

In most American cities, a student enrolled in the public school system is assigned to a local school by the district. Parents do not usually select the public school that their child will attend. In recent years, however, a growing number of citizens have backed reformers' efforts to allow parents to choose their children's schools. Such "parental choice" alternatives include open-enrollment options, which allow parents to send their child to any public school in their state; charter schools, which are publicly funded schools operated by parents and teachers; and voucher programs, in which parents are given state-funded tuition grants to send their children to private schools.

Choosing the best option for your child is complicated and can be intimidating. Unfortunately, just dropping children off at the neighborhood school without a second thought isn't always the best choice anymore. Since choices do exist, it's important that we become educated about them. The following chapter will cover several school choice options.

School choice is the slogan of a U.S. movement to give parents more say in which primary and secondary schools their children attend. The movement hopes that increased choice will cause more fierce competition between different schools and thereby raise the overall quality of education.

School choice proponents differ in the extent to which they advocate privatization. Some don't advocate it at all, wishing only to allow parents greater choice between different public schools within a district. Others seek to blur the distinction between public and private schools by granting parents the option of either spending vouchers at private (or possibly religious) schools or getting tax credits for doing the same.

The proponents of school choice say that if parents are given a choice about where public money should go, they will pick the better schools, and the underperforming schools will have to improve or lose public funding. Proponents claim that school choice is a good way to improve public education at low cost by forcing schools to perform more efficiently.

Critics argue that tax breaks and vouchers will take away money from the schools that most need financial assistance and that taking money away from them will make those schools' position even worse.

Proponents of school choice believe that empowering families with educational options will promote change in how school systems are governed.

Choice has been widely adopted. Hardly a state in the United States does not have some type of choice plan and hardly a major urban area does not have a limited choice plan.

In 1988, Minnesota became the first state to enact statewide open enrollment for all students, making all public schools throughout the state open to any K–12 student, provided that the receiving school had room and the transfer did not upset racial integration efforts.

Students also have numerous other options. High school juniors and seniors can take courses at public or private institutions of higher education for both high school credit and college credit. Dropouts and students at risk of not graduating are offered supportive programs. In addition, families are allowed to claim a tax deduction for school expenses, including private school tuition. The Charter Schools Act permits teachers and parents to create and operate new public schools, which are accountable to public authority and parents.

New York City has citywide choice. The largest public school system in the nation consists of thirty-two community school districts serving nearly 1.5 million highly diverse students. Parents have the right to transfer their children to any New York City public school, provided space is available. A well-known choice district is District 4, which lies in East Harlem, one of New York City's poorest neighborhoods. Teachers were given the autonomy to redesign schools and even create new schools. Orientation sessions are offered to parents who are interested in enrolling their children at these schools.

Many districts throughout the nation offer the choice of magnet schools. Students have the choice of academic or vocational magnets or those that combine academic and career programs. These schools have programs that focus on science and engineering, medicine, the performing arts, the humanities, law, business, fashion, or other themes. Parent and staff involvement increases and the students appear to be highly motivated.

Choice in Massachusetts has been seen as a means to achieve racial and ethnic balance in the schools. Experiments with choice grew out of efforts to attract white students into inner-city schools. The family selects a school after receiving information, and an assignment is made based on family preferences. All students have equal access to all public schools regardless of geographical location.

Cambridge has one of the most successful choice programs in Massachusetts. The crux of the program is the Parent Information Center, which offers information in six different languages. Students in Cambridge outperform students nationally in reading, math, social studies, and science (Cambridge Foundation, 2004).

Milwaukee, Wisconsin, implemented the nation's first pilot voucher choice plan in September 1990. Selected students are entitled to receive public money to attend any nonsectarian private school of their choice. The cash value of the voucher is equivalent to the state per-pupil expenditure on public schooling. Parent involvement in school activities was greater in choice schools than in most other Milwaukee public schools (Witte, 2004).

Choice, as shown in the above districts, has proven to be a useful tactic in promoting urban public education transformation and experimentation, and its focus on the involvement of families in all phases of schooling is important.

Inner-city parents and church pastors have joined together with residents of rural areas and homeschoolers in demanding greater educational freedom. Educational vouchers, tuition tax credits, charter schools, and other forms of school choice have garnered the support of a diverse coalition of parents in search of a common end: educational excellence. Public education bureaucrats and many teachers' unions remain vigorously opposed to greater educational freedom and the competition and accountability it brings. With reform, they would see their monopoly power vastly diminished in favor of parents and children.

The ideal form of education is one that is freely chosen by parents in accordance with their values, which best meet their child's intellectual, physical, and spiritual needs. Religious and private nonsectarian schools can play an important role here as a free market in education allows a wide variety of school concepts to take hold. The most efficient system of education would be one that resembles the free market for other goods and services, with many providers to meet the diversity in needs.

Through school choice, parents learn to become more actively involved in the decisions surrounding their children's education. They are no longer forced to remain passive figures in the lives of their children, with government bureaucrats remaining to call the shots. Instead parents are called upon to "shop around" for the best available education in order to meet their child's needs. Parents exemplify responsibility in taking such an active part in their own child's education. This is something that would have been next to impossible for many parents, especially for low-income parents whose children are most in need of a sound education in order to realize their full potential later in life, without a school choice regime.

More questions arise: Do educational vouchers permit government officials to regulate the religious activity in schools, or simply enable parents to purchase an education at the school of their choice? Do tuition credits allow social engineers to encourage one form of educational experience over another, or simply enable parents to better afford the education deemed by them most appropriate for a child? Are the freedoms of charter schools dramatically imposed upon by bureaucratic restrictions, or are these publicly funded schools superior to the present system of public schooling?

These are valid concerns that must be examined as the evidence on school choice continues to pour in. A school choice regime that only entrenches government in education, instead of freeing parents from bureaucratic control, is self-defeating and sows the seeds of its own demise.

Advocating school choice is a way to achieve greater liberty and parental responsibility in education. School choice in all its many forms is a prudent step in the right direction: toward restoring the fundamental role of parents in providing an education for their children.

More and more over the last few years, public school systems have been providing parents with a range of choices for their child's education. As previously stated, these choices include transferring to another school within the district; becoming part of a school with a special focus like math and science, often called a magnet school; participating in a charter school or alternative school; attending a private school; homeschooling; and in some cases providing vouchers, providing the parents money to allow their children to enroll in a private school of their choice.

What should one consider when choosing a school option?

There is a lot to think about when choosing the right school for your child. Whether you are moving him or her to a new school or simply choosing a school for him or her to start in, it is a big decision. How do you know which option is best for you? Consider the following.

- Class size: The number of children in each classroom may make a difference in how much your child is able to learn.
- School size: Some children do better in large schools where they have many other children to play with and many choices for classes. Others like smaller schools, where there are fewer choices for classes and closer relationships with students and teachers can be made.
- Subject matter: Some schools are able to concentrate on specific subject areas, such as sciences or arts, more easily than others.
- Location: The location of a school is important to some parents and students for reasons of safety, convenience, and facilities.
- Test scores: The highest test scores are not always a guarantee that a school and its teachers are good, but they do indicate that children at the school learn more over time than children at schools with lower test scores.
- Diversity: To some parents it is important for a school to be racially, ethnically, and culturally diverse.

How do you research your school options? In addition to the factors listed above, you need to understand each option before making a decision. One such option is transferring to another public school, choosing to move your child to another public school, perhaps in a different neighborhood than the one they live in or go to school in now. You may find that another public school in a different neighborhood is a better place for your child to learn. Schools are different in different areas, so it is important to look at other schools and find one that matches your child's needs. For example, if your child works better in small groups, look for a school that may have smaller classroom sizes, even though it is a few extra miles away.

Another option is public charter schools. These schools are public schools that are granted a charter or contract to operate as if they are independent for a period of time (usually three to five years). During the contract period, charter schools are given freedom from regulations that other schools may have to follow. In return for this freedom, charter schools have to produce positive academic results, or their sponsors may choose not to renew their charters.

Magnet schools are an option. Magnet schools are specialized schools within the public school system that attract certain types of students. Many magnet schools have good reputations for teaching students, especially in their specialty areas. Students in magnet schools are surrounded by students who have interests similar to their own. Some magnet programs are whole-school magnets where all students in the school participate in the program. Others are programs within a larger school setting.

The voucher program is a fairly new option. A voucher is a letter that represents money. The voucher is given to parents to allow them to send their children to a school of their choice. Publicly funded voucher programs use money that would normally go to the regular public schools in order to pay for the costs incurred in going to a private school or a religious school or homeschooling.

Homeschooling is another option, and the states allow parents to educate their children at home rather than in public or private schools. Parents appear to homeschool for a variety of reasons. Most are unhappy with their child's school and feel that they can do a better job than the current school. Some parents do not like the school environment and think there is too much violence or other social issues and want to protect their children from those situations. Some parents choose homeschooling to foster a closer family unit. Some children do not learn well in a classroom setting and learn better at home. Homeschooling is a lifestyle and a commitment. Once you decide to homeschool your child, you have to prepare the assignments, plan the classes, and teach and assess your child. It takes a great deal of time and commitment on your part.

You may choose a private school because you are concerned about your child's religious education and send them to a parochial or nondenominational Christian school. You may want a certain standard of advanced education that your local public school just can't offer, or your own experience in a private school was such that you hope to duplicate that positive experience for your child.

Next you must prepare your child for a new school.

Changing schools is a big deal. It means making new friends, meeting new teachers, and going to a different building and area. Help your child to know what to expect. For example, check out the bus route or subway route prior to his or her first day. It is important that children feel safe and know where they are going. Talk to your child about being in a new place and meeting new people. It is tough to start anew. Help your child find out what is expected of him or her, how grading works, and if the workload is different. Encourage him or her to stay active by playing a school sport, joining band or choir, and continue doing activities he or she likes. Finally, find out if other children in the same class live close by and try to meet them so your child sees a familiar face that first day at school.

We all have goals for our children. We all have our own philosophy of education. Our actions are a result of what we believe. What kind of person do you hope and pray your child will grow to become? His or her schooling choice should nurture that goal and not hinder it.

If your child is currently enrolled in school, you can ask yourself some critical questions to determine whether or not the school furthers the goals you have for your child. Be grateful choices exist. It may have seemed easier when there were no choices with regard to schools, but it wasn't always better. Some of our children have greater needs than their neighborhood schools can meet.

Choices create competition, which raises the level of excellence. Choice is a good thing. One of the beauties of choice is that nothing is written in stone. You can always choose again if circumstances or needs change.

What does your child really need?

Your child's needs are the pivotal pieces in your decision making. Family needs are also a big piece of the pie. What is your child's preferred learning style? What are his or her gifts and talents? Matching your child's education to your child's needs and learning style creates harmony. It decreases frustration and lowers stress levels for all concerned.

If your child is a strong visual learner who is also spatial and needs to move around as he learns, a traditional classroom with a lecture format for teaching will make him or her squirm. He or she will only absorb snippets of information. The better you know your child, the better able you are to make the best choice possible for him or her. We tend to put more effort into buying a house in just the right neighborhood with the right amenities (based on family needs) than we put into choosing our child's schooling.

Where children go to school can be an emotional decision. A step-by-step process can take the anxiety out of the decision making. First, define the problem. It can be difficult to put our finger on what exactly is wrong, especially when we are upset. Try to see the real problem in the mess. Next, brainstorm possible solutions or alternatives. Judge them according to whether or not they can solve your problem. Let your creative juices flow and don't censor your ideas—let them come. Develop a plan of action and be prepared to adjust the plans when necessary. Always ask yourself if the mission of the school matches the specific needs of your child, if parent involvement is highly valued, and whether or not the values of the school are in line with the family values.

When looking at private schools, ask yourself if the curriculum is appropriate and challenging enough for your child, if the teachers are certified in their subject areas, if the learning environment nurtures creativity or stifles it, and how much homework is required weekly.

If you are planning to homeschool, ask yourself if your child is ready for school at age five, socially as well as emotionally. Are you willing to sacrifice your time, give up that alone time to always have children around? Do you have beliefs or values to impart, and are you willing to learn? No matter your background, it takes commitment, love, and the willingness to learn what works and what doesn't work for your child.

Another question you must answer for yourself with regard to school choice is: "What is my philosophy of education?" Schools are created and managed with an emphasis on a particular educational philosophy. Sure, there is always talk about what should or shouldn't be taught in schools. Everyone is concerned about the values imparted. But as you consider where to place your child for seven (or more) hours per day, you must also consider the philosophy from which the school is operating.

What is the purpose of education? Answer the question for yourself and then use the answer to help you choose the right school for your child. Your philosophy should match the school's as closely as possible. The following are some directions that schools take in their own philosophies. Find out which one you are considering among the following. It is one more piece in the puzzle.

- Outcomes-based education (OBE): The intent here is to judge schools not by what goes into them, but by what comes out of them, namely, how much and how well children learn.
- Education standards: Standards-based education argues that students are apt to be better educated if those in charge are clear about what exactly the students are supposed to learn.
- Skills versus Knowledge: This thinking scorns the idea that students must master certain facts. The argument is that since knowledge is changing so fast nowadays, there is no reason to memorize any of it.
- Multiculturalism: This stresses the importance of children developing knowledge of a number of different cultures and a respect for other people's heritages.
- Developmentalism: This view says that children develop in natural stages at their own pace, and that learning should never be forced on a

child. You may hear the term "developmentally appropriate practice" in preschool and primary classrooms. It means that if a lesson is taught too soon, it will be a waste of time or even detrimental to the student.
- Cooperative Learning: This idea encourages teachers to divide a class into small groups of students who work on assignments together. The group demonstrates what it has learned, and everyone shares in a single grade.

Parents are empowered through school choice. There is no longer any debate over whether parents want choice (they do) and whether they are more satisfied with their child's education once empowered to exercise choice (they are). Mounting research shows that parents both want to and know how to make informed choices for their children's education. Studies from school choice experiments, including the Milwaukee Parental Choice Program, Dayton Parents Advancing Choice in Education (PACE) Program, New York School Choice Scholarship Program, San Antonio CEO Horizon Scholarship Program, and Washington Scholarship Fund, show that choice can be an engine for parental involvement.

These studies indicate that parents with children in choice programs attend more school activities, volunteer more in their children's schools, communicate more with teachers, and help more with homework.

On virtually every measure tested (school safety, discipline, instructional quality, teacher skills, respect for teachers, class size, and school facilities), parents are overwhelmingly more satisfied with their chosen school than their assigned school. Parents are also more likely to reenroll their child in the chosen school because of their satisfaction with the program.

Americans want to see choice implemented. A survey by Portrait of America in 2004 found that 52 percent of adults believe that introducing competition by allowing parents to select schools would do more to improve education in America than spending money. Similarly, 54 percent favor school vouchers, and 59 percent say that allowing parents a choice in school selection is more likely to produce accountability than oversight by a school board. For years, polls have shown the vast majority of voters favor school choice programs. Even parents who say they wouldn't change schools if they could believe parents should have the choice opportunity.

The public education system, not public school teachers or administrators, is the greatest barrier to parental involvement. It interferes with the parents' right and responsibility to seek the education they believe is best for their children, and the monopolistic practice of directing all public funding to public schools has fostered indifference among parents, many of whom feel little reason to pay attention when their choices are made for them.

If all parents had the financial ability to choose their child's school, those schools would survive only if they placed students' interests before all else.

Teachers and administrators would have to improve their schools through the healthy competition that would evolve in a choice system. More important, school choice places higher expectations on parents.

Today it is fashionable to hold parents responsible for cultivating their child's educational and social progress, but parents have limited authority outside the home to fulfill that duty. Choice frees parents from the shackles of bureaucratic control and increases their ability to participate in their child's overall development.

School choice often comes under fire from teachers' unions. Dire union warnings broadcast that allowing parents more educational options could spell the end of public schools. However, there is a strong constituency of people who believe greater school choice will actually improve education. And as for teachers, there are many reasons to believe that choice will benefit them too. Let's look at the arguments. Critics of school choice argue that allowing more students to leave the public schools will result in teachers being laid off or becoming unemployed. But a moment's thought reveals a flaw in this argument. Demand for teachers will not decrease just because more parents choose to send their children to different schools. And these different schools are likely to be in the same general area of the schools that the students are leaving. So if jobs are lost at the old school as a result of a mass student exodus, the new schools still will need to hire teachers to meet their demand.

There is even the possibility that greater school choice would result in more jobs for teachers. How? As competition among schools intensifies, administrators will need to come up with ways to attract more students. One of the selling points many schools employ is that of smaller class size. As more schools offer smaller classes as an incentive to parents, more teachers will be needed to keep the teacher-to-pupil ratio low.

Another claim of school choice critics is that choice will necessitate many changes that are disruptive to the educational process. True, but that can be a good thing. Teachers are used to adapting to new situations. They have a new batch of students every year, sometimes twice a year. They adapt to innovative teaching methods and ideas all the time. Sometimes this happens formally with training and in-service, but more often it happens informally. A teacher picks up a new idea from a colleague, a magazine article, a parent, or even a student. The "disruptions" caused by school choice will only enrich the cross-fertilization of ideas, to the benefit of the students.

Choice programs can allow teachers to improve and do their jobs better. Most teachers agree that new ideas and new situations are what make their jobs exciting and fun. Too many teachers tell stories of how they've been pressured, if not intimidated, into altering or abandoning something they believed in because of bureaucratic interference.

When school choice forces schools to listen to the teachers, that means teachers will be a part of the changes that will inevitably occur.

Finally, critics argue that school choice will mean pay cuts for teachers. This is an unlikely scenario. The private sector pays more, and since school choice money follows the students, parents who can afford several thousand dollars a year in tuition under a voucher or tax credit plan will find themselves in the private school market. A lot of that new money will go to teachers as competing schools scramble to attract and retain the best educators they can find. Teachers do not need to fear school choice. The evidence shows that it will benefit them as well as their students.

Genuine competition is our best hope for a better K–12 education system. In a truly competitive setting, public and private schools would compete equally for customers. Parents would be able to choose equally among public and private schools.

Currently, school choice programs appear as nothing more than escape valves for low-income children trapped in the worst inner-city schools. We should seek school choice for all children. The dream of creating a higher standard of quality for both private schools and public schools can become a reality, but only if we set a goal of a choice system that will improve government-owned and private schools.

Desperate times require desperate measures. Can we learn a lesson from Martin Luther King as the school choice battle gets intense? It will take action, not armchair radicalism, to convince policymakers that parents really want more educational choices. King outlined the steps for nonviolent social change. School choice advocates should look to these steps for guidance. Step 1 is information gathering. King wrote that those who want to make social change should look at the facts to see if social injustice exists. In 1963 America there clearly was injustice against blacks. It is clear today that many public schools fail to provide a quality education for many (not a few of whom are black Americans). We have all seen the data showing that 55 percent of blacks and 53 percent of Hispanics graduate from high school, compared to 81 percent of whites (*Education Week*, 2006).

Step 2 is negotiation. Start discussions with the status quo. In school districts around the country, parents have complained about schools that have failed to educate their children. Some of them, who do not want to negotiate with the system, have fled to private schools or decided to try homeschooling. Step 3 is self-purification. This step asks participants to consider what their level of personal commitment will be. What are parents willing to do to demonstrate their demand for school choice?

Finally, step 4 is direct action. The civil rights movement used several types of direct action: sit-ins, demonstrations, and boycotts. King said that he agreed with his critics that negotiation is better than direct action, but, ironically, it is direct action that leads to negotiation. The beauty of school choice is that it is a form of direct action. Once parents have school choice, they will no longer have to negotiate or renegotiate with a recalcitrant status quo.

Like Martin Luther King with his civil rights struggles, school choice advocates need to heed the words of Frederick Douglass, who said, "If there is no struggle, there is no progress."

Locally and nationally there is increasing, many-sided concern over the state of American education. From crisis in the inner cities to general academic underachievement, to ethical relativism, to remoteness from parental control, to burgeoning bureaucracies and bloated budgets with corresponding tax burdens, educational problems confront us. And there is a growing perception that these problems reflect the monopoly-financing environment out of which they have come. That monopoly artificially protects the public schools from normal competition and comparison, thus encouraging bad habits, and it endangers independent schools cut off from normal funding. Thus, public schools suffer in terms of educational quality, and independent schools suffer, often unto death, from underfunding.

And just as the vices of monopoly funding are becoming clearer, so is the ability of choice to break the monopoly and help rid us of its vices. By permitting parents to allocate tax dollars, choice would end the monopoly of assignment. In the same motion, it would reestablish parental control and introduce comparison and competition, the normal human stimuli that encourage excellent performance and cost restraint.

Add to these facts the truth that choice has no downside risk, since any positive educational idea can be explored under it. After all, it is simply "nature taking its course" in education. Parents free to choose without financial penalty will choose schools, public or private, which they judge best for their children, and a natural variety of educational options and models will arise, reflecting America's pluralism.

When the contemporary school choice movement started several years ago, its leading protagonists probably could have met comfortably in a telephone booth. In an amazingly short period of time, it has grown into one of the most sophisticated, passionate, and ecumenical movements in American history. I've never encountered a group of people, activists, philanthropists, public officials, clergy, lawyers, teachers, and parents who are so motivated by good faith and willing to put aside ideological differences in pursuit of a common cause. That is probably why the movement has come so far so fast.

The school choice movement has widespread, diversified political appeal. Reasons for this support include: given the right circumstances, it enables low-income and minority families to avoid poorly run and overcrowded schools; it infuses free market, competitive principles into a sluggish public educational system, it allows individual families, not bureaucratic school systems, to have more control over which schools their children attend and what services are provided there; it is considered a low-cost solution to what are considered enormous problems in public education; it is purported to lead to better matches between pupil needs and school offerings, and it may increase parent involvement in education.

The school choice struggle has been fought on many fronts. The decisive battles have come in the courtroom, yet whatever the legal issues in a particular lawsuit, our core argument throughout has been that parents, not government, should have the primary responsibility and power to determine where and how their children should be educated.

The stakes are enormous. For the education establishment, the cause is about jobs and power. For the parents, and for society, the stakes are much higher. Over half a century after *Brown v. Board of Education*, nearly half of all black and Hispanic children in inner-city schools have much greater likelihood of winding up on welfare or in jail than going on to college or productive lifestyles. That is because our K–12 system of education, especially in large urban centers, is a government monopoly much more responsive to special-interest demands than satisfying consumers. Until we alter the distribution of power, we will consign additional generations of children to educational cesspools. In climbing out from this morass, we should not worry about whether a particular reform proposal is too radical; we should worry about whether it is radical enough.

At its essence, the school choice movement is a civil-rights crusade, an effort to vindicate the sacred and unfulfilled promise of equal educational opportunities. It is not just about ideas, but also about the real lives of real people. Over the years, I've met hundreds of low-income parents in cities across America. Many are single parents; few have high school diplomas, let alone college degrees. But they know that in order for their children to succeed, they must somehow secure for them a high-quality education. Unfortunately, the system has written them off, both parents and their children. Too often, the public schools are hostile to low-income parents and assume that they are part of the problem, not part of the solution. The schools assume the children are incapable of learning and subject them to low expectations.

In alternative schools and private schools, both parents and children are transformed. The parents are not discouraged from involvement—they are required to play a role in the school and in their children's education. The students are expected to behave, and expected to achieve, and they do. I've walked the hallways of dozens of inner-city alternative schools and visited private schools. The biggest difference is in the children's faces. Regardless of the obstacles they face in their lives outside of school, they are kids who are going somewhere. That look of self-confidence, of determination, of earned pride is all the fuel, all the reward that I could possibly desire.

School choice will not single-handedly solve all education-related problems, for example, uneven resource availabilities and broken and dysfunctional families, both of which make the dream of a level playing field for all children difficult to achieve. But educational choice is an obvious and inevitable cure for much of what ails us.

In our media-intensive culture, it is not difficult to find differing opinions. Thousands of newspapers and magazines and dozens of radio and television talk shows resound with both differing points of view. The difficulty lies in deciding which opinion to agree with and which "experts" seem the most credible. The public needs to be offered a choice of ideas even more than a choice of schools.

Thomas Jefferson once stated that "difference of opinion leads to inquiry, and inquiry to truth." You must examine the facets of school choice (charter schools, magnet schools, private schools, homeschooling, vouchers, etc.) and examine them with skill and discernment. The choice is yours.

7

Rethinking Issues in Educational Reform

You can't teach a child how to think unless you have something for him to think about.

—Georgann Reaves

Educational reform is certainly not a new idea, but it has been gaining momentum in the last twenty years. International economic developments, wars, conflicts, terrorism, and technological advances are among factors that have been identified as having powerful effects on our national educational system. Such forces, when interpreted through the lens of American economic resources, policy-making processes, and educational values, have caused the American public to examine their educational system with increasing regularity. The result is the need for educational improvement.

At the heart of the debate are issues such as educational equity, staying in school, standards, assessment, leadership, motivation, and the students themselves. We are now at the point where we need to take a very serious look at the roots of public education and question the very structure of its existence. Thus was born the movement toward the restructuring of education.

In the past, the press for attempts, even haphazard or one-sided, at reform has been a result of the public quick-fix mentality, one directed at curing the perceived ills of schools in response to concerns of our competitiveness among industrial nations.

The news has been devastating. U.S. high school graduates are not able to perform entry-level tasks in the new workplace. International studies continue to show the United States to be well down the educational list by almost every measure. The world has changed, yet the United States has steadfastly held to the structure of the industrialized society of the late

nineteenth and early twentieth centuries. We still train our students to pas-
sively accept the information given and to react with a uniform feedback
method. In the industrialized society, workers were to perform, not think.
In the technological society, critical thinking is the expectation and team
solving is the norm. We have even held onto a remnant of the agrarian society, the summer recess during which students would help on the farm. The
conclusion is obvious. We are educating today's students with the schools
of yesterday for the world of tomorrow.

Let us now look at some of the issues facing reform today. It is my belief
that our school reform system is the most fundamental cause of the social
problems that our society faces today. Our most critical mental attributes
involve emotions, judgments, a sense of priority, empathy, conscience, interpersonal relationships, self-esteem, identity, independence, the ability to
concentrate, and a number of others.

There appears to be a sharp jump in the incidence of mental illness immediately after children begin school. This would suggest that something
about our school system is in direct conflict with the human psyche.

By restructuring our schools, many such disorders can be prevented. Let
me explain. First we must conquer our obsession with attempting to align
academic achievement with a timetable. Everyone has a very unique personality, and therefore, learns at a different pace. Some children are ready
to learn how to read at age three, while others may be better suited to learn
how at age ten. In schools, we force subject matter down the throats of the
students. We neglect to realize that children learn much more quickly and
effectively if they are receptive and eager to learn the subject matter.

Forcing children to learn has no value and may be extremely harmful.
Grades, busywork, and competition are at the core of the problems that
plague our schools. The motivation to learn must come from within the
student. As a child, everyone is curious and eager to learn. Before attending
school and being subjected to this process of coercion, children manage
to learn a complete language (in bilingual families, two languages) and
a copious amount of things about their environment. There is no reason
why such learning could not continue without the negative effects of rigid
institutionalization and standardized test scores, which seem to form the
basics of modern-day education. Rather than hindering the growth of our
children, we must provide an environment that will nourish them and facilitate continuous learning.

In order for students to reach their fullest potential, they must be allowed
to develop their own individual educational programs. Teachers should be
present to facilitate this process and should be available when called upon
for help by their students.

In our schools today, two of the most neglected areas of adolescent
development are the social and emotional aspects. Children need to exist

in a healthy community that is open, honest, nurturing, interactive, and free from harmful activities such as bullying, humiliation, favoritism, and scapegoating.

As I have previously stated, all children have unique personalities and therefore will all respond differently to various educational methods. Rather than the stagnant classroom environment that currently exists in many of our schools, classrooms would become places for workshops, discussions, laboratories, and other activities. Talking, movement, and experimentation would be encouraged rather than forbidden. There is no reason why discussion groups could not exist in high schools, middle schools, and even elementary schools. A variety of discussion groups where students could express their feelings openly would be valuable at all levels in our educational system.

Students would be able to attend the activities of their own choosing. Learning would be made an active rather than a passive endeavor. In this process we, as educators, must help students prioritize their needs and interests, extract relevant facts from complex realities, make judgments and decisions based on facts, communicate effectively, and empathize and feel emotional connection with others.

Part of our job is to teach our students to be in touch with their feelings and be aware of their strengths and weaknesses in order to think independently; to be conscious of more than black and white and to allow for the gray. We also need to lead our students to develop the ability to focus their thoughts on an objective while tuning out irrelevant distractions, temporarily ignore the extraneous distractions of the world, and focus on what truly matters to them.

I see poor decisions made by administrators, curricula that lack relevancy, and staff that blame and punish rather than attempt to understand. I see educators who hang on to the clutter of the past and thus have difficulty moving forward. Our current school system, government-controlled and factory-like, provides an environment that promotes this.

The teacher says that you will learn what I want you to learn and do the many assignments that I give you or you will be in big trouble. Students want to learn, not be controlled. Excessive assignments and busywork do not work for very many students. Teachers stick to textbooks without animating the printed words through the use of demonstrations and examples. There are teachers who suppress any student effort to introduce innovative and creative ideas into the classroom, because such additions deviate from the curriculum they use.

There are administrators who are unwilling to transform an obsolete educational system for fear of harming their vested interests. They have sacrificed the qualities of humor, empathy, judgment, and even humanity in their pursuit of power and control. They lack the wisdom to know the difference between what they can change and what they cannot. They may manipulate and use other people, deny responsibility, and blame others. These people are the products of our present educational system.

Our schools can do a great deal to promote change. We need to abandon rigid requirements and courses that are of marginal value. We must weigh the time, energy, and cost of a program against its future value.

We must stop trying to exert too much control over the lives of the students. It is critical that children be able to develop in ways that are consistent with their own unique personalities. The system must conform to the needs of its students, not vice versa.

Should we shift the role of the teacher from lecturer to educational manager? We can remove the excessive busywork and homework. We can spend more time listening and less time giving instructions. Children, even very young children, have an instinctive sense of what they need.

We need to bridge the gap between the classrooms and the outside world. Remember, learning can take place outside of school just as effectively as it can in school. It is also important to give students credit for past or present outside work experiences.

How about endorsing the notion that every person has value, no matter what his or her walk of life? Our academic system often discriminates against students who have an aptitude for trades. If a child wants to pursue a trade, he or she should be encouraged to do so, rather than be coerced into changing his or her mind.

Finally, we often hear teachers complaining that they can't control their students. The solution to this problem is to stop trying to control them. Education should be an invitation, not an issue of force.

The stimulus in learning should take the form of a question, which leads one to think about an answer. This can lead to self-initiated exploration and finally a feeling of success.

Low morale among students should be met head-on. Many feel their work is meaningless and has no lasting value. We need to do more than just memorize data, pass tests, and forget. We need to develop creativity and eliminate the biggest obstacle to developing creativity, which is fear. We need to replace fear with independence, real-world relevance, skills for earning a living, teachers who care, and adults who listen. As I've said, children need to be in control of their lives. For some reason, our educational system can't seem to break out of this rigid straitjacket. Each one of us must take responsibility for change.

Rather than diploma mills that stress rote memorization, schools could become learning centers where students would be allowed to study their choice of a variety of courses, the subjects that interest them most. Teachers could become facilitators, guiding when requested.

In the richest country in the world, children have lost their instinctive passion for learning and life itself. We must promote change. Did you know that William Lear of Learjet fame was a high school dropout? Pierre Cardin and Liz Claiborne, fashion gurus; the founder of McDonald's; the founder of Wendy's; Benjamin Franklin; and one in every fifteen millionaires—all were dropouts. What does this say for our educational system?

Ask any group of teachers what they wish for at the beginning of the school year and don't be surprised if they answer, "A classroom full of students who want to be there and are motivated to learn and succeed." However, in the real world of teaching, motivation levels among students can vary widely.

Too often we are dealing with students who don't want to be in school, aren't interested in learning, don't believe they can succeed, and don't get involved in what we are teaching. There they sit, bored, watching the clock, staring into space, and feeling lost and hopeless. These unmotivated students avoid challenges, refuse to complete assignments, and seem satisfied to just get by. They slack off if the subject is boring to them, can't focus, believe that mistakes mean they are not smart, and have been lost since day one.

These students leave you feeling frustrated because what works to motivate other students simply does not work for them. They drain your energy because they demand so much extra time and effort on your part. They challenge your authority, disrupt your class, push your buttons, and sometimes make you wonder why you would bother with them at all, when so many other students do want to learn.

But it doesn't have to be that way. You can start dealing positively with any difficulties you've encountered in motivating students, including those who have lost interest and hope. You can become the spark that ignites the flame in every student in your classroom. Your unmotivated students probably won't change on their own. They need you to put the wheels in motion.

We must determine why students don't care, choose discipline methods that increase the desire to learn, and ask the right questions to draw students out and then into the lessons. Let's make routine tasks fun and all the while convey love and caring. Students who have goals are focused on meeting them, take responsibility for their own actions, are curious about the world, and are motivated to try and therefore learn.

So much is at stake when it comes to the difficult job of keeping students motivated: your students' academic future and your personal reputation.

Motivating and challenging the unmotivated learner involves renewing the desire in every student, even those claimed to be "lost causes," to try and succeed; implementing positive discipline strategies that make students who want to throw in the towel want to try; understanding why some students don't care and how teachers often contribute to the problem; recognizing conditions in your classroom that interfere with learning; and avoiding rules and procedures that zap students' desire to learn.

We are now realizing that at every level, learning must be connected and integrated if it is to be perceived as relevant to the learner. As the walls of tradition begin to crumble, we have found that a teacher-advisor program, which connects each student with a caring adult, helps with motivating students. Add a life skills curriculum, cooperative learning, and social skills awareness leading to working as a team and you are on your way. In order for a person to be motivated, it is clear that the end result must be worth the effort. If we want our kids to become motivated about school, then we must remember that everyone is motivated by something. We just need to discover what each student needs from us and then create an environment where learning is exciting for everyone. We should also strive to build strong, caring relationships. Students will work harder and take more learning risks with people they trust if we convey a sense of "we are all in this together," which builds camaraderie and leads to success.

In our national discussion, there is perhaps some confusion between what schools offer and what students learn. Some tend to see education as something that adults do to children. It really is still fairly common to hear talk about schools "delivering education" to students. This mindset makes it fairly easy to believe that there is some one "effective intervention" that would work with all students.

These notions should set off warning bells for policymakers. They could take the country down a track that would not lead to the achievement of our national goals (the NCLB goal of all children being proficient in terms of high state standards by 2014). Their effect could be to drive up the quit rate, reducing both high school graduation and college admissions. Indeed, something like this might already be happening. Large numbers of students are leaving school or, while not physically leaving, are not engaged or learning.

This failure is now appearing in the statistics. California denied forty thousand diplomas in June 2006 to students who did not pass its achievement test, and in the state of Washington, thirty-two thousand students from the class of 2008–2009 have not yet passed a math test required for graduation. Students are demoralized and think it is useless to go on, and are dropping out of school (Blankinship, 2006). Confronted with this failure, states are tempted to try to "game" the accountability system in order to make student performance appear better, if not putting off the "high-stakes" tests, lowering their passing scores, or fudging on the promised consequences of failure.

The country needs to think critically and soon about whether its effort to improve learning would perhaps be more likely to succeed were the focus to shift from accountability requirements to student motivation. Policy-makers and educators should consider approaching learning as a voluntary act, as something that students do, encouraged and assisted by adults.

In Minnesota, a member of former governor Rudy Perpich's staff used to correct people who talked about farmers growing corn. "No," he would say, "farmers do not grow corn, farmers help corn grow." The distinction is subtle yet fundamental. Students learn. Teachers help students learn. Motivation matters.

So the effort to improve learning has to engage the question of whether school motivates students. When learning was optional, motivation was irrelevant. But now that learning is considered imperative, motivation becomes essential. Thus, if NCLB is especially about helping the now-not-learning youth to learn, we need to ask whether the current strategy, built on the notion of increasing rigor and raising standards, can alone achieve that end. I believe that in our national effort we now need to think much more about how students look at conventional school and what kind of school they want to attend that will motivate them to learn.

In June 2006, *USA Today* released a story that shocked no one who knows the major statistics about education. In an Editorial Projects in Education Research Center study, Christopher Swanson found the nation's overall graduation rate to be 69.6 percent, based on 2004–2005 data. That means 1.2 million of the established 4 million eligible to graduate each spring are not likely to complete school. Swanson's study suggests that students who are not completing high school may be disproportionately from large, urban school districts. Three of the nation's fifty largest school districts are graduating fewer than 40 percent of students "on time and with a regular diploma." They are Detroit (21.7%), Baltimore (38.5%), and New York City (38.9%) (Toppo, 2006).

According to Jay P. Greene, senior fellow at the Manhattan Institute for Public Policy Research, the nation has not made much progress toward improving its school completion rates in the past three decades. Greene reports that the United States has had a national graduation rate of about 70 percent since rates peaked at 76 percent in 1979 (Greene, 2006).

Effective strategies for addressing the 30 percent national high school quit rate are the subject of an intense national dialogue. Adults engaged in the dialogue do not often have the perspectives of the youth who are doing the questioning. Adding their perspectives to the conversation is necessary.

So let's ask the students who were once on the path to quitting. The students I interviewed identified ten common factors as being inversely related to school completion. They are lack of motivation; lack of personal attention from teachers, counselors, and/or administration; teaching strategies that are not challenging, interesting, interactive, or culturally relevant; poor academic performance; absenteeism; personal circumstances not conducive to school participation; limited access to resources that would aid learning during nonschool hours; unstructured discipline and attendance policies; bureaucratic processes; students sensing they were not respected or feeling stigmatized, discriminated against, and powerless to be heard.

Manuel, in tenth grade, said, "I think people ditch because they get frustrated because the teachers don't take the time to go over things that they don't understand." Salina, also in tenth grade, said, "The teachers don't care, some don't even know my name." Dionte, a twelfth-grader, said, "I don't get any attention because everyone recognizes the smart kids." Charles said, "I was by myself. No one came and asked how I was. I went off into the cracks. They gave up on me."

Emotional and social support would lessen the barriers to school completion. Juan, a twelfth-grader, reported that he stayed in school (p.m. program) because the coordinator of the program became a role model, friend, and parent figure for him and helped motivate him when he needed it.

Several students said they want more challenging work: "They let you pass anything you got." One said, "Teachers are lazy and just ask you to turn in any old work. I ditch because the class is boring." Sherice said, "They make you take classes in school you are never going to use in life."

Others spoke about failing and missing too many days. One parent said, "Schools shouldn't wait so long to communicate. My son didn't attend for twenty-three days before they finally called me."

The students interviewed said that they worry about living, how to get money, and how their mothers are going to survive. They said if they were lucky enough to find a job then the school made it more difficult. The girls spoke of not having child care available ("Taking care of my family comes first.") We must consider these factors in our dialogue.

Participation was a huge issue for all students interviewed. The students sensed that adults did not respect their humanity, made judgments based on race (security guards treated students of color more harshly than whites), looked down on foster-care kids or group home kids, and that they were stigmatized because of their past mistakes even after they took active steps to get back on track toward graduation.

What we have seen in the comments of these students suggests that a wide variety of factors can influence school completion. It seems some will be motivated by increased rigor and standards, and some will not. Many will be motivated by interactive curricula while others look for personal relationships. Any school will be hard-pressed to accommodate all of the students in one setting, but we can individualize and try. If we were to make motivation central to educational policy and school design, educators influencing K–12 education might find ways to customize this concern.

Minnesota is encouraging the creation of new and fundamentally different schools that can tap into the motivations of students who are not sufficiently motivated in conventional settings or by rigor alone. According to October 2008 data provide by the Minnesota Department of Education, almost 18 percent of all public school students enrolled in Minneapolis and St. Paul school district boundaries are attending the area's sixty-four charter schools. As more charter schools open and district enrollment in the Twin Cities declines, the population of students attending charter schools is growing rapidly. This suggests there is a need and a market for fundamentally different schools.

"Staying In" became the theme song for two very special students who were on a path to quitting school. Listen to their stories as to why motivation was central to their learning and graduating.

Codie Wilson, a self-described "former gangbanger" and ward of the State of Indiana, went from having failing grades in a traditional Indiana public school to receiving As and Bs at St. Paul's chartered High School for the Recording Arts (HSRA). Codie's grades earned him the opportunity to take advantage of the school's partnership with local music production company Studio 4. Recording and producing music was a motivating factor that Codie openly acknowledges "saved his life" and led to his 2003 high school graduation and his current mission to help other young people achieve the same turnaround in their lives that he experienced at HSRA. With the skills and confidence he gained in school, Codie is currently working on his fourth CD and getting ready to release his third. He is also performing regularly. In addition, Codie also works at HSRA, where he can be a mentor and resource for students. Codie is proud that he can now use his experiences at HSRA and his music to positively influence and give hope to other young people who are facing problems like the ones he once had.

Travion Allen is an American Indian and African American who went from believing he was "a dummy who didn't know nothing" to feeling like a math genius after receiving extra help from his teachers and principal and after learning through culturally relevant curriculum that his capacity to make a contribution to society is far greater than he once thought. After graduating from Oh Day Aki Charter School on time in 2008, he will attend one of three colleges (University of Denver, University of Minnesota, or Minneapolis Community and Technical College) to which he has already been accepted. Travion believes the culturally relevant curriculum is important to offer all American Indian students, who he says frequently have difficulty rising above society's low expectations for them. Adults at Oh Day Aki are trying to show American Indian kids that you may have dropped out in the past, but in the end, if you go to school, all the stuff you learn stays with you, and the kids feel like they are somebody. In an effort to make sure students know that they can succeed in college and beyond, Oh Day Aki has formed partnerships with institutions of higher education to constantly expose students to campus life and the college application process. For Travion, the culturally relevant curriculum and having access to a large amount of academic and social support from adults helped him to believe that he could not only learn well, but could one day use his talents to improve society.

The varying circumstances and motivations of today's young people suggest there is no silver bullet that policymakers and educators can use to improve school completion rates and help all students learn. The reality is that students will decide for themselves whether or not they will achieve academically. That is true for all people who are told to do something. We should expect, even accept as a premise in our decision making about education policy and school design, that we will need to appeal to motivation if we want our kids to attend school, learn, and graduate.

The trouble is, when it comes to students learning, many decisionmakers influencing education have the mindset that they can control student learning. Adults who feel this way set rigorous standards for all students and expect that learning will improve simply because students are required to meet these standards for graduation. These same decisionmakers believe that students who need more or less flexibility should just adapt to conventional settings. At the same time kids, their families, and other activists generally acknowledge student differences but frequently expect that schools must be the ones to accommodate the needs of every student.

Logically speaking, neither the decisionmakers' nor the families' one-size-fits-all expectations are achievable. Students are not likely to adapt, and schools are not likely to accommodate everyone. Accommodating different students will require that legislators and educators find ways to customize learning so they will be able to tap into the varying motivations of those who are not learning well. We may need to consider a parallel strategy of creating unconventional schools for different kids. With options available, kids will find that learning can be customized to their individual needs and motivations. Because these new and different environments exist, some kids who once faced obstacles to graduating are attending schools of their choice and are learning both academic and life skills. If we help these same kids to understand the world in which they live today, they will develop the capacity to succeed tomorrow. We can help them use and develop disciplinary knowledge and consider the questions they need answered through the lens of today.

Traditional textbooks do not work anymore. They become obsolete before they reach the classroom. Fortunately, a curriculum based on current events has a ready-made ongoing text that contains the ideas of our time. When students learn to think critically about today, they will develop the ability to approach tomorrow and the preparation for tomorrow with insight and curiosity. These are the greatest gifts we can offer our students.

Are we ready to tackle the next major issue in the realm of educational reform? We can't escape the term *standards*. I've always been wary of the term. The origin of the word itself connotes a dormancy or inertia: a standing still. As an educator and administrator, I've been told that standards are our friends, that we need them to ensure program quality, to indicate our goals, and to promote systems change. To my mind, the imposition of guidelines set by anyone beyond us seemed superfluous and a bit intrusive. I've viewed standards as a bureaucratic constraint devised to restrain creative teaching, foisted upon teachers in the field in the name of greater program accountability. Standards implied uniformity and a universality borne out of the K–12 educational mainstream. (The model that failed learners in the first place.)

Well, that's what I thought over the years. However, in the process of looking more closely at my teaching practice and my administrative expertise, I have come to realize that a standard doesn't require subservience to just one curriculum or instructional method, but can inform and improve them. A standard just might involve an internal awareness more than an external encroachment. A standards-based approach might just recast programs favorably by allowing us to show more authentically what to do. Standards should allow us to view knowledge and skills in the context of students' lives. A multitude of paths help us to explore the framework, and lessons can be presented from a number of different perspectives. Standards work when they codify our internal values and respect our individuality. There will always be tension between the specific student and the general rule. Standards should work when they encourage dialogue between these realms.

Congress and President Bush made a bold and historic promise when we pledged in NCLB that the federal government would do all in its power to guarantee every child in America, regardless of race, economic background, language, or disability, a chance to get a world-class education. We are making progress toward fulfilling that commitment. Before the act was passed, most states lacked ways to track student progress and teacher effectiveness. Today all fifty states have standards, assessments, and accountability procedures that enable us to track the achievement of every student. Every school measures performance, based on progress in closing achievement gaps and getting all students to meet high standards. Goals, standards, curriculum, and assessment are intricately tied together. Standards are meant to be the anchors.

But to fulfill our promise, much more remains to be done. We continue to have problems. Whenever we talk about raising standards, we can't seem to agree on what the standard is or should be or has been. Therefore, we need to strengthen our academic standards and assessment methods to ensure that students have the knowledge and skills necessary for today's global economy. We must expand and fortify the teacher workforce. Teacher quality is a critical factor affecting student achievement. Good teachers can make all the difference in closing achievement gaps for low-income students and students of color. However, our most at-risk students are often taught by the least prepared, least experienced, and least qualified teachers. Standards simply do not tell teachers *how* to help their students attain them. There is no guidance on the process of their implementation, which means teachers themselves must translate the language of standards into instructional practice. Finally, we shouldn't label schools inadequate, we must help them improve.

Standards: what are they? Standards have been one of the hottest topics in education reform for more than two decades. The drumbeat has been fed by fears that American kids, the future American workforce, are not keeping up with their peers in Western Europe and Japan. During these years, raising standards in the major curriculum subjects has gained momentum across the country. Academic standards make clear what students should learn and what teachers should teach, making the educational system accountable for results.

Setting standards has gradually generated agreement about the meaning of two key concepts, academic content standards and performance standards. Content standards describe what every student should know and be able to do in the core content areas (math, science, language arts, and social studies). Most of all these content standards should apply equally to students of all races and ethnicities, from all linguistic and cultural backgrounds, both with and without special learning needs. Performance standards answer the question, "How good is good enough?" They define how students demonstrate proficiency in the skills and knowledge framed by states' content standards.

The ultimate success or failure of standards-based reform rests heavily on the creation of new forms of assessment—specifically, new performance-based assessments. We need to include a variety of forms, including complex tasks, investigations, portfolios of student work, project-based learning, and so on, that require learners to make use of prior knowledge, recent learning, and relevant skills in actively solving significant and realistic problems.

Will standards solve our educational problems and make American students world-class academic performers? The question has generated fierce debate among K–12 educators. Opposition to standard-setting efforts has been intense and often effective (e.g., rejecting a system of national tests). Nonetheless, despite setbacks, the standards movement marches on and seems to be gaining ground.

We can't discuss standards without assessment. So, what are promising ways to assess student learning?

If you cared about improving students' capabilities, you would design assessments to make individuals aware of their progress. You would design them to demonstrate what students are learning and what they can do with their knowledge by performing in some way by writing, demonstrating, explaining, or constructing a project or experiment. As an educator, you would interpret the results to spark reflection and then suggest approaches for further development.

What distinguishes some newer assessments from some traditional forms is that assessment, curriculum, and investigation are intertwined. Two strategies come to mind: projects, which are extended performance tasks that may take several days or even several weeks to complete, in which students generate problems, consider options, propose solutions, and demonstrate their solutions; and portfolios, which are collections of student work that show teachers and others who may "score" portfolios the range and quality of student work over a period of time and in various content areas. Ideally, portfolios capture the evolution of students' ideas and can be used instructionally and as progress markers for students, teachers, and program evaluators.

However, in many schools and departments of education today, we have come to rely on a single measure for evaluating student progress: conventional, standardized tests. These tests, including most state-level tests, only measure formal knowledge. The results arrive after months of delay, often after students have moved on to another grade level. They display only one or two highly aggregated scores, giving students limited information about their skills. By showing only the percentage of items that students got wrong, they subtly lead students to feel that their skills are inadequate, which goes against the grain of what we know about learning. (Start with the strengths of a person's work and then move to where the student needs improvement.)

Assessment of student achievement is changing, largely because today's students face a world that will demand new knowledge and abilities. In our current global economy, students will need to understand the basics but also need to think critically, analyze, and make inferences. Helping students develop these skills will require changes in assessment at the school and classroom level, as well as new approaches to large-scale, high-stakes assessment.

Assessment is slowly changing for many reasons. Changes in the skills needed for success, in our understanding of how students learn, and in the relationship between assessment and instruction are changing our learning goals for students and schools. As society shifts from an industrial age, in which a person could get by with basic reading and math skills, to an information age, which requires the ability to access, interpret, analyze, and use information for making decisions, the skills and competencies needed to succeed in the workplace are changing as well. In response to these changes, content standards (the knowledge, skills, and behaviors needed for students to achieve at high levels) are being developed and reviewed at the national and state levels. Policymakers reasoned that if schools and students were held accountable for student achievement, with real consequences for those that did not measure up, teachers and students would be motivated to improve performance. Ironically, those effects on classroom instruction have often narrowed the curriculum and limited learning opportunities available to students.

In this atmosphere of reform, student assessment is the centerpiece of many educational improvement efforts. Assessment reform is viewed as a means of setting more appropriate targets for students, focusing staff development efforts for teachers, encouraging curriculum reform, and improving instruction and instructional materials.

Many educators and policymakers believe that what gets assessed is what gets taught and that the format of assessment influences the format of instruction. Contrary to our understanding of how students learn, many assessments, especially traditional multiple-choice and true-false assessments, test facts and skills in isolation, seldom requiring students to apply what they know and can do in real-life situations. Standardized tests do not match the emerging content standards, and overreliance on this type of assessment often leads to instruction that stresses basic knowledge and skills. Basic skills and minimum competencies become the overarching goal of schools and teachers and do not help the students achieve.

However, educators, policymakers, and parents are beginning to recognize that minimums and basics are no longer sufficient and are calling for a closer match between the skills students learn in school and the skills they will need upon leaving school. In fact, schools are now expected to help students develop skills and competencies in real-life, "authentic" situations, and schools are expected to graduate students who can demonstrate these abilities.

As we look at current assessments and design new ones we should be aware of the following: align assessments to agreed-upon standards of student performance; give support to teachers and schools in changing they way they do business by eliminating assessments that are aligned to shortsighted, outdated goals; look closely at timelines, since we can't wait weeks for feedback; be honest and realistic and face the need for change; use reflection and self-evaluation; allow for constructive guidance with a focus on the evidence; and allow for the parents to be involved, since they are the best advocates for their children.

In addition, we need to not only be interested in the answers our students know, but also closely observe them when they don't know the answers. Watch for the following characteristics: persistence (use of alternate strategies for problem solving); decreasing impulsivity (using more reflection); listening to others and showing understanding and empathy for other points of view; and gathering data through all senses.

We must also consider that any assessment of student achievement is unlikely to exert influence on instruction unless some stakes are attached to its results and teachers value the assessment as an accurate reflection of what students know. High stakes come in many forms, including tangible rewards, sanctions, or public comparisons of students and schools.

We cannot forget that as a group, racial and ethnic minority students score lower on traditional assessments than do white children, in large part because they are more socioeconomically disadvantaged than white students. Will a switch to alternative assessments close the achievement gap between the two? The new assessments may not, by themselves, remove the systematic barriers between these groups, but we need the chance to find this out.

Under the current system, racial and ethnic minority students are disproportionately represented in remedial and lower-track classes because of their poor performance on the standardized tests, which determine placement in these classes. Teachers in these classes report spending larger amounts of their time on test preparation and teaching basic skills and less time on higher-order skills than teachers in higher-performing schools. Socioeconomic isolation puts them at a comparative disadvantage to their white peers.

This reality has educators now focusing on a new concept of equity in relation to the introduction of alternative assessments. We must carry equity beyond just giving students equal opportunity to achieve at a higher level. We must make sure each student gets the support and resources needed to master high-level content. Schools have no choice but to reform their efforts toward increasing low-achieving students' exposure to high-level content. The first step is to address inequities in the current educational system. There is little reason to believe that alternative assessments will help if only a privileged few are exposed to the content they assess.

None of the issues mentioned previously can be dealt with unless we consider the role of leadership in this reform process. "Strong leadership" appears on virtually every list of attributes of successful schools. But what do long-term school reform leaders view as their essential professional competencies? What do leaders see as their role in sustaining reform? And how do they engage teachers, families, and communities in partnerships that build programs to help children meet challenging standards? By identifying key dimensions of leadership for sustaining reform, we can answer these questions.

We need to look at partnership and voice. Effective reform leaders cultivate a broad definition of community and consider the contribution that every member can make in order to help children meet challenging standards. They hear the voices of many stakeholders and establish partnerships that permeate all aspects of reform.

Vision and values are important: effective reform leaders are dependable and committed "keepers of the dream," and keeping of the dream means adopting key values. Good leaders know that the dream must be student-centered and focused on ambitious academic goals and that the dream is continuously evolving. An effective principal needs to have the capacity to inspire in others the sense of commitment and passion that will carry change over the long haul.

Knowledge and daring are two important pieces of the leadership role. Effective reform leaders develop relevant information bases and cultivate human resources to minimize failure while encouraging risk taking. They study, count, seek advice, send staff to workshops, bring in experts and mentors, consult, and increase their capacity to make good decisions. They step into the unknown and encourage staff to do likewise.

Savvy and persistence come next: effective reform leaders know how the system works, and they can take a lot of flak (if they must). They know how the school and structure nurture or discourage attitudes and behavior. They can put up with resistance and find ways to win cooperation. They are great managers as well as leaders. Most of all these principals and leaders maintain a network of supporters to lean on in times of stress.

Finally, effective reform leaders put to good use an array of personal qualities that make leadership more effective (passion, humor, empathy). Strength of character and maturity are also essential. Patience is key. Good leaders have both wisdom and common sense and are viewed as trustworthy and reliable. "If you are not sensitive, you have no business working and dealing with children," says a colleague.

In addition, self-assessment is a tool effective leaders use to demonstrate their accountability to their own values. Some leaders keep journals for reflection. Others develop portfolios of selected work. Some use surveys. All effective leaders tend to rely on "critical friends" or mentors.

Like any other assessment, self-assessment has three components. First, am I doing a good job? The answer reflects what a "good job" looks like. Second, data collection must be relevant, practical, and accurate. Third, techniques for analyzing data should make technical sense, and choosing a strategy that matches one's learning style or circumstances makes a lot of sense. The appeal of self-assessment is that it permits us to create an accountability system tailored to our avowed principles and situation. Competence in designing and implementing self-assessment plans should be a central element of our professional development.

American society has faced a number of rapid changes—the advent of an information society, globalization, an increasing birthrate, and an aging population. These developments have led to calls for the transformation of the country's educational system. Educational reform is linked to the issues mentioned in this chapter. Successful implementation of reform requires the fullest possible support of the public at large. Diverse views are bound to emerge. Doubts and criticisms will be voiced. There are many hurdles to overcome in the educational reform process.

Presently, we are bound by NCLB. NCLB is not just a slogan. It's a national commitment, inspired by our fundamental values and aspirations. It's a promise to do all we can so that every American child receives the high-quality education he or she needs and deserves. We may never achieve that lofty goal, but if we hope to keep America strong and just, prosperous and free, we can never stop trying.

8

Role of Poverty in School Reform

To hell with the cheese, let's get out of the trap.

—a mouse

Pedro lived on a trash-littered, half-demolished street behind an entry door with busted locks, up four flights of a graffiti-covered stairwell that smelled of urine, in an apartment that had unreliable heat and hot water, windowpanes that rattled in the wind, and lots of old woodwork painted dark brown, the favorite color of landlords.

Inside the apartment lived a transvestite uncle of Pedro's and his sixty-nine-year-old grandmother, the person he called mother. "I also got four stepmothers," Pedro explained. "My father never gets married with women. He don't like it. I got a whole lot of brothers and sisters, all with different mothers." Pedro didn't know how hard his life was, but he soon would figure it out, and the comfort dispensed by drug dealers would be waiting for him. Pedro needs help *now*!

A battle quietly rages in America, and our kids are caught in the crossfire. It's a war of philosophies, a battle of worldviews on poverty and radical agendas (world government versus national sovereignty, group-oriented discovery versus individual knowledge-based learning, and the federally mandated NCLB versus local control of our schools).

We must ask ourselves this question: do our schools exist to educate the child and to transmit our culture, or do schools exist for the purpose of making our children into political activists on behalf of a new vision of what some believe our country should be?

We also ask: what role, if any, does poverty play in education?

Consider the kids coming from an inner city that is characterized by fatherless homes, poverty, high crime rates, gangs, and who are often English as a second language learners. What kind of magic wand do schools have to raise every member of this group to a high level of academic proficiency? How can our nation provide superior educational opportunities for all students?

The future of our children, the future of our nation, is in our hands. Don't ask someone else to fight on your behalf. Be willing to do whatever is necessary to ensure academic excellence for all students. In order to ensure a viable future, educators must tackle the issue of poverty and how it affects the education of the nation's children.

In the 1960s and 1970s, when the legal foundations of social justice were getting firmer, public schools across the United States were getting worse. It became apparent that underachieving schools hold back disadvantaged children, especially those living in poverty, disproportionately, because low-income homes are typically less able than advantaged homes to compensate for the knowledge gaps left by the educational system. The overall decline in the quality of education/schooling will thus have an uneven social effect. All children, including those of the middle class, will be poorly educated, but the negative effects will be strongest among the least privileged. As children from impoverished neighborhoods advance through the grades, they will accumulate relatively less intellectual capital than they would have under a more demanding educational system. Educational injustice will grow, whether or not the schools are racially integrated.

Since inferior education is today the primary cause of social and economic injustice, the struggle for equality of educational opportunity is in effect the new civil rights frontier. This new struggle is more subtle and complex than the earlier one of sit-ins and freedom rides. In this struggle, it is harder to tell good from evil, true from false.

When we talk about school reform, we can't avoid the issue of poverty. I firmly believe that poverty is associated with academic performance. Poverty restricts the expression of talent and the success of children as compared with middle-class students. Medical problems also appear to affect impoverished youth and limit academic achievement as well as life chances. I have also noticed that small reductions in family poverty can lead to increases in positive school behavior and better academic performance. Poverty places severe limits on what can be accomplished through school reform efforts. We must look closely at the issues of poverty with regard to our schools.

Looked at from afar, there are basically two main factions when it comes to thinking about education these days: those who think underlying problems of poverty and race need to be addressed before significant improvements can be made in education, and those who believe that schools can get much better at helping children learn within the current reality.

When thinking about how to alleviate poverty in the inner city, we must distinguish between those who believe you have to change the attitudes and behavior of the poor before they will be able to thrive economically and those who believe that the poor need decent jobs and other resources before their attitudes and behaviors will change.

In both cases, the distinction turns on the source of the problem. Roughly speaking, is it underlying societal problems or is it the behavior of the participants, specifically school systems and poor inner-city residents? If not one or the other, the question becomes one of priorities and focus.

I'm hardly an expert on poverty, but based on what I have read, it seems that we still don't know how to answer that question for poverty, but seem to have a pretty good idea of how to answer it for education.

The recipe for how not to be poor is simple: avoiding long-term poverty is not rocket science. First, graduate from high school. Second, get married before you have children, and stay married. Third, work at any kind of job, even one that starts out paying the minimum wage. And finally, avoid engaging in criminal behavior.

How do we change attitudes? Middle-class women in their early and mid-twenties want to get married someday, when the time is right, when careers are underway. Poor women tend to see marriage as a luxury, something they aspire to, but fear they might never achieve. However, they judge children to be a necessity, an absolutely essential part of a young woman's life, the chief source of identity and meaning.

In education, on the other hand, several schools (a small but growing number) are proving that with high expectations, a rigorous curriculum, and dedicated teachers and principals, low-income black, American Indian, and Hispanic students can excel. Many of these schools are charter schools, which have considerable freedom from government control. These schools are succeeding because they are tackling the poverty issue.

Unless more schools are freed from the constraints of the traditional public school system, the racial gap in achievement will not significantly narrow. School choice programs are the very programs that may enable poor students of color to break out of the cycle of poverty we are all concerned about.

THE PROBLEM

If you step back and take a look at schools in the United States, you may notice one very important thing: something is not right and it needs to be changed. Many schools in the United States just are not living up to the kinds of schools such a well-developed and rich country should have. Many politicians are putting all the blame on the schools. If the schools fail to produce, many will be taken over or even closed down due to the No Child Left Behind Act. If we start to break down all the data, all the test scores, and many other factors, we notice one very important fact: many of the schools that are failing are schools in impoverished communities, filled with poor students of color. Looking at this, I cannot help but think that maybe the schools themselves are not completely to blame.

I think there is a correlation between poverty and poor school performance. Just think about this for a moment . . . Are your parents educated? What income class did you come from? Do you think coming from a lower or higher income class could have changed your education? These are questions reformers should take a look at. Poverty is a major problem and a problem that needs to be addressed to better reform and further the educational system in the United States.

LIFE OUT OF SCHOOL

One very important aspect in which children of different socioeconomic backgrounds differ is in their life out of school. An estimated five thousand hours per year are spent outside of school versus nearly one thousand hours in school. It is hard to believe that the students' lives outside of school do not have an effect on their education. Experiences in the day-to-day lives of students from various socioeconomic classes will differ.

Parents/guardians are some of the most influential people in every child's life. I think the parents are the first step in educational reform. The parents need to encourage their children to finish school and need to do their best to ensure that their children are given every opportunity possible to succeed. The problem is that many poor children's parents are uneducated and may not know the best way possible to help their children. This is something I think the war on poverty should focus on. Most parents seem to love their children and want to give them all the opportunities that they have never had. The parents are a very important factor in determining what happens to their children and I think they should be treated as such. If parents are unable to give their children proper help themselves, we should at least let them know how to lead their children to help.

Friends, other peers, and other family members are another very important factor in every child's life. Other people's opinions and views can have a huge effect on a child's actions. Some students in lower-class neighborhoods are seen as trying to be white by their peers if they try hard to succeed in school. That is a horrible way to view success. Just think of the psychological impact that may have on children. They do not want their peers to have a poor view of them, so they may stop trying to succeed in school altogether. A statement like that could potentially destroy any motivation that child had to succeed, especially for a young child.

VIOLENCE AND DRUGS

Another important thing to consider is the high rates of violence, ethnic conflict, and drug use in high-poverty areas. Everyone knows that these areas are potentially very dangerous, as are the schools in these neighborhoods. Many white suburbanites are scared to go to the ghetto for fear they may be shot on sight. (Television news clips support this.) In reality, this may be unlikely to happen, but violence and ethnic conflict do remain a grim reality.

ETHNIC CONFLICT

In New York City, two African American students and later a Hispanic American student were attacked by white students. Their faces were stained with white paint. In Chicago, African American and Hispanic American students engaged in gang warfare. As a result, thirteen students and one teacher were injured. Sixty teenagers were arrested. In Minneapolis, the Native Mob, an American Indian gang, was involved in robberies of several homes in their community. Ethnic conflict remains a huge issue linked to our schools, especially inner-city schools, and our communities of color. These actions are linked to issues of poverty.

The economic decline that America has experienced in the past few years has also fueled racial and ethnic conflict. When jobs become scarce and competition for them increases, people are more likely to resent members of other ethnic groups. People going through hard times want to pin the blame for their difficulties on someone. Schools are quick to point out an increase in racial tensions when the economy worsens.

As we attempt to reform our schools, we must look for ways to resolve and even avoid conflicts. Young people may be powerless in turning the economy around, eliminating poverty, or changing the political climate, but they can do something about the level and content of their education.

Before something can be done, schools must admit a problem exists. Once you do acknowledge a problem, follow-up actions that make it clear prejudice, discrimination, and acts of hate will not be tolerated. Antidiscrimination policies, cooperative learning, multicultural education, prejudice reduction programs, and peer mediation are ways we can help resolve ethnic conflicts head-on.

We must also take into consideration gangs and drugs when dealing with poverty. There appears to be a rise in gang activity and membership. This brings about an increase in acts of violence and fights. Many fights now involve the use of guns and other weapons.

In an area in the South Bronx in New York City, gunshots ring out daily. The *New York Times* calls this place the deadliest precinct in the city. Eighty-four people were shot on a street called Beekman Avenue in the past two years. Over half of these deaths were of people under twenty-one. It was reported that in a thirty-minute span in 2006 there were three people shot and killed on this street (Berliner, 2006, p. 54).

The problem of gangs is difficult to crack. Students join gangs for a variety of reasons. Some join because it becomes an issue of economics. Times have been hard recently, and gangs make money, by stealing and selling or by drug sales. The most common reason for joining a gang, however, is a need to feel a sense of belonging. Single parents, whether mothers or fathers, may have to work two or three jobs, and when they do get home, they are too tired to want to spend time with or deal with their children. Gangs provide the missing sense of family.

Drugs are also born out of poverty. In many large urban centers cocaine and heroin addiction are commonplace. Many of the heroin ("the needle drug") users are infected with HIV. Most of the children of these neighborhoods know a relative or neighbor that died from or is dying from AIDS. Many young women tested in obstetric wards are positive for the disease and pass it on to their unborn babies. Fear and anxiety are common side effects.

Where do the schools fit into this picture? Once again, the role of poverty is all around us. Because of this, the school community has to squarely acknowledge the problems involving poverty and move ahead to conquer them. We need to become inspired, not discouraged.

As I researched these stories, I realized how lucky I am not to be in one of these places. I cannot imagine worrying about school with things like that constantly going on around me. As I was growing up, I never worried about being shot or felt unsafe going to school. I can also say that I never heard a gunshot growing up that did not involve hunting or a shooting range. I suspect circumstances are similar for most suburban children or those in small rural towns. It is very hard to put myself in others' shoes and imagine what life would be like in South Bronx or the barrios of Los Angeles. However, I have no doubt that if I had grown up in an inner-city neighborhood, steeped in poverty, I would not have attended college, and even graduating from high school would have been a much greater challenge.

When you see pictures and read about kids that sleep in sleeping bags in hats and coats on a December night, in very cold weather, with little or no heat, you can't help but react. In the summer, these same kids have roaches and rats crawling all over the place. Who wants to concentrate on math when you are freezing or having roaches surrounding you? These conditions are horrific. These images really help us to see why poverty can make learning a very difficult challenge.

STILL SEGREGATED THROUGH POVERTY

In 1954, the United States Supreme Court declared that segregation in schools was illegal and against the very principles on which this country was founded. It is 2008 and the nation's schools are still, even after fifty-four years, segregated by race. In the 1970s and 1980s there were many attempts to desegregate schools, but most of them failed. The desegregation movement lost most of its momentum in the 1990s. Not to mislead anyone: it is against the law for a school to refuse a student solely based on race. Our schools are not solely segregated based on race; it just so happens that most of the schools that serve impoverished neighborhoods happen to have mostly students of color due to the fact that people of color make up the majority of the low-income people in our country.

The achievement gap between white and black students appears to be getting larger. When we look at eleven-year-olds, only one in every one hundred African American students is able to read and interpret technical data, compared to one in twelve for European Americans. Similar results are found when looking at the ability to solve math problems. At the end of high school, African Americans read and do math at a level similar to most eighth-grade white Americans. When we look at other test scores and similar data, the results tend to be the same (Ipka, 2008).

Many years ago, Martin Luther King Jr. made many statements supporting desegregation. He said that segregation harms not only the segregated, but the segregators as well. Some believe diversity makes for a more valuable educational experience for all students. Many are against this belief. Ask yourself, if its supporters are so for it, why are they not fighting to better integrate K–12 public schools? Nothing will magically happen if nobody is doing anything about it.

Here is something to really think about: nearly half of all African American and Latino students drop out of high school. The percentage is even higher for American Indian students. These figures are ridiculous and embarrassing. How is this even possible in a time when the importance of school is stressed so much? We all know that graduating high school is the first step in securing a bright future.

These dropout and graduation rates are unacceptable. We also should not have this great achievement gap that we see year after year. Why do students of different races seem to do so poorly in school? Many people believe that poverty is the key. We cannot let these kids not get a quality education and continue the vicious cycle of poverty. If we can get these kids the same opportunities as their suburban peers, who knows what they can accomplish and will be capable of. Education is quite possibly the key to stopping poverty permanently. But to give these low-income students the needed education, we may first need to give them a boost out of poverty.

Let us now analyze the role of poverty in school reform. Several points can be addressed. First, poverty in the United States is greater and of longer duration than in other wealthy nations. Second, poverty among urban children/ families of color is associated with academic performance that is well below international means on a number of different international assessments. Scores of low-income students are also considerably below the scores achieved by white middle-class American students. Third, poverty restricts the expression of genetic talent at the lower end of the socioeconomic scale. Among the lowest social classes, environmental factors, particularly family and neighborhood influences, not genetics, are strongly associated with academic performance. Among middle-class students, genetic factors, not family and neighborhood factors, most influence academic performance. Fourth, compared to middle-class children, severe medical problems affect impoverished youth. This limits their school achievement as well as their life chances. Impoverished neighborhoods do have a negative effect on the youth who reside there. Fifth, small reductions in family poverty lead to increases in positive school behavior and better academic performance.

It is argued that poverty places severe limits on what can be accomplished through school reform efforts, mainly those associated with the federal NCLB law. I suggest that the most powerful policy for improving our nation's school achievement is a reduction in family and youth poverty.

I do not believe that NCLB is needed to tell us where those failing schools are located and who inhabits them. By ignoring the effects that poverty has on our failing schools we severely limit our thinking about school reform. Poverty has powerful effects on education, and we can't escape it.

Many educators and teachers understand, though many politicians choose not to, that school reform is heavily constrained by factors that are outside of America's classrooms and schools. Although the power of schools and educators to influence individual students is never to be underestimated, the out-of-school factors associated with poverty play both a powerful and a limiting role in what can actually be achieved.

It is not important to argue about the fine points at which poverty is miserable or barely tolerable, or whether a person is stuck in the lowest of the social classes or merely belongs to the working poor. We know well enough what we mean when we speak of poverty, communities of poverty, the very poor, and the like. We also know that the lower social classes and the communities in which they live are not all homogenous. It is a simplification, and therefore a mistake, to treat a group as if the individuals who comprise that group are the same.

It seems to me that in the rush to improve student achievement through accountability systems relying on high-stakes tests our policymakers and citizens forget, or cannot understand, or deliberately avoid the fact that our children live nested lives. Our youth are in classrooms, so when those classrooms do not function as we want them to, we go to work on improving them. Those classrooms are in schools, so when we decide that those schools are not performing appropriately, we go to work on improving them as well. But both students and schools are situated in neighborhoods filled with families, and in our country the individuals living in those school neighborhoods are not a random cross section of Americans. Our neighborhoods are highly segregated by social class, and thus also segregated by race and ethnicity. So all educational efforts that focus on classrooms and schools, as does NCLB, could be reversed by family, could be negated by neighborhoods, and might well be subverted or minimized by what happens to children outside of school. Improving classrooms and schools, working on curricula and standards, improving teacher quality, and fostering better use of technology are certainly helpful, but not the only answer.

It seems ludicrous to me that most of what we try to do to help low-income youth is classroom- and school-based. Education doesn't just take place in our schools. It is a fact of contemporary American life that many of the poorest of the children who come to our schools have spent no time at all in school-like settings during the first five years of their lives. And then, when of school age, children only spend about thirty percent of their waking hours a week in our schools, and then for only two-thirds of the weeks in a year. You can do the arithmetic. In the course of a full year, students might spend just over one thousand hours in school, and almost five times that amount of time in their neighborhoods and with their friends and families.

For all youth, those five thousand hours require learning to be a member of one or more cultural groups in that community, learning to behave appropriately in diverse settings, learning ways to get along with others, and learning to survive on the streets, to fix things, to think, and to explain things to others. These are natural and influential experiences in growing up. But for poor kids, ghetto kids, what is learned in those settings can often be less helpful. It appears that many of the families in these impoverished neighborhoods are so poorly equipped to raise healthy children that the schools those children attend would have a hard time educating them even if they weren't also so poorly organized and operated.

It has become increasingly clear that several decades of educational reform have failed to bring substantial improvement to schools in America's inner cities. The public needs to be aware that the structural basis for failure in inner-city schools is political, economic, and cultural and must be changed before meaningful school improvement projects can be successfully implemented. Educational reforms cannot compensate for the ravages of society.

When we speak with directors of inner-city schools, we hear that relatively few urban poor students go past ninth grade, and the graduation rates in large comprehensive inner-city high schools are abysmally low. For example, Oakland, California, has been reforming its schools since 1973. Oakland's educators are not ignorant or uncaring, and neither are Oakland's parents. But, to date, no one in Oakland and elsewhere has been able to fix Oakland's public schools. Is that because we are looking for keys in the wrong places?

As educators and scholars, we continually talk about school reform as if it must take place inside schools only. We advocate for adequacy in funding, high-quality teachers, professional development, greater subject implementation, cooperative learning, technology-enhanced instruction, community involvement, and lots of other ideas and methods. Some schools in our most distressed areas do show some success, but success often means bringing the students who are at the twentieth percentile in reading and mathematics up to the thirtieth percentile in those skills.

Many schools feel technology is a major player in school reform. In fact, a discourse of reform claims that schools must be transformed to take full advantage of computers, while a competing discourse of inequality warns that technology-enhanced reform is taking place only in the wealthy schools, dooming poor students and students of color to the wrong side of a digital divide.

As educators cope with the task of integrating information technology into the schools, two main discourses have appeared: the discourse of reform and the discourse of inequality. The discourse of reform suggests that schools must transform themselves in order to make effective use of computers.

It has been proven that the infusion of new technologies produces little result if underlying relations do not change. The root of the problem appears to be a mismatch between industrial models of schooling and the postindustrial organization of society. The solution should include not just diffusion of technology in the schools, but rather the creation of new models of interactive, autonomous, student-centered learning, which allow students to use technology in a process of critical, collaborative inquiry (when the teacher's goal is to empower students as thinkers and problem solvers).

While the discourse of reform is hopeful, the discourse of inequality fueled by poverty is troubling. From this perspective, increased use of technology in the schools is bound to heighten distinctions among students based on class, language, and race. A teacher colleague in Hawaii explained, "I see this change to technology as creating two classes of schools: those who can afford the technology and those who can't. The rich schools will get richer and we are going to create a greater divergence between our best educated students and our poorest educated students." The discourse of inequality focuses on the fact that low-income students and students of color have less access to new technologies or are more likely to use them for rote learning activities.

Inequality falls into at least three areas: home access (wealthy families are much more likely than poor families to own a home computer), school access (schools in low-income communities had limited Internet access and had a large number of students per computer), and use within schools. (African American, Hispanic, and American Indian students are more likely to use computers for drill and practice, whereas white and Asian students are more likely to use them for simulations or applications. The same differences appear between poor students and wealthier students.)

Putting the discourses of reform and inequality fueled by poverty together causes two scenarios to emerge. The dream scenario is that the Information Age will help bring about the kinds of educational change that reformers have pushed for, with schools becoming sites of critical collaborative inquiry as individuals and small groups work with new technologies to solve authentic problems under the guidance of a facilitating teacher. The nightmare scenario is that this type of educational transformation will occur only in elite private schools or wealthy suburban schools, with urban and rural poor attending schools that either lack computers or use them in the most traditional and ineffective ways.

The truth will probably lie somewhere in between. Not all wealthy schools will use computers for the best interests of their students, and not all poorer schools will use them badly. Nevertheless, there are a number of factors that make the nightmare scenario all too likely, including the depth of already-existing inequality in U.S. schools, the heightening economic polarization in the United States in recent years, and a history of a hundred years or more in which learner-centered reforms have almost always been implemented more readily among privileged students than among students of poverty.

Perhaps we are not doing well with our urban schools because our vision of school reform is impoverished. It is impoverished because of our views on how the role of the government should play out, our beliefs about the ways in which a market economy is supposed to work, our concerns about tax rates, our religious views about the elect and the damned, our peculiar American ethos of individualism, and our almost absurd belief that education is a cure for whatever ails society. These well-entrenched views that we have as a people make helping the poor seem like some kind of Communist or atheistic plot. Some reference the myth about the power of the public schools to effect change.

Other educators and policymakers note that it is hard to think of a more satisfying solution to poverty than education. Many feel the poor can overcome disadvantage on their own. Our myth of individualism fuels the school reform locomotive.

On the other hand, the idea that schools cannot cure poverty by themselves sounds something like a vote of no confidence in our great American capacity for self-transformation, a major element in the stories we tell of our American nation. But is educational inequality rooted in economic problems too deep to be overcome by school alone? Schooling alone may be too weak an intervention for improving the lives of most children now living in poverty.

Those who blame poor children and their families, and those who blame the teachers and administrators who serve these kids and families in our public schools, are all refusing to acknowledge the root problem contended with by too many American schools, that poverty is an issue that must be dealt with.

Instead policymakers almost universally conclude that existing and persistent achievement gaps must be the result of wrongly designed school policies: either expectations are too low, teachers are not qualified, curriculum is badly designed, classes are too large, school climates are too undisciplined, leadership is too unfocused, or a combination of the above.

Americans have come to the conclusion that the achievement gap is the fault of "failing schools" because it makes no sense that it could be otherwise. This common-sense perspective, however, is misleading and dangerous. It ignores how poverty and social class characteristics in a stratified society like ours may actually influence learning in the schools.

For decades, the association of social and economic disadvantage with a student achievement gap has been well known to economists, sociologists, and educators. Most, however, have avoided the obvious implication of this understanding: that raising the achievement of lower-class children requires the improvement of the social and economic conditions of their lives, not just school reform.

The United States is among the leaders in childhood poverty among the rich nations. The poverty we see among children is not random. It is unequally distributed across the many racial and ethnic groups that make up the American nation. New immigrants, African Americans, Latinos, and American Indians, particularly those among those groups who live in urban areas or reservations, are heavily overrepresented in the groups that suffer severe poverty.

The United Nations Children's Fund (UNICEF) report on child poverty (2005, p. 8) also reminds us that there is a charter about the rights of children to which 192 United Nations (UN) members have agreed. It is sad that many member nations sign such a charter and then do little to live up to it. But still, at the very least, signing is an acknowledgment of the underlying concept, and only two nations have refused to sign this charter. One of the nations is Somalia. Can you guess which is the other nation? You guessed correctly if you chose the United States of America. We will not sign a charter guaranteeing the rights of already born children, though we somehow managed to get a bill through our Congress that guarantees the rights of unborn children.

Apparently we, the American people, do not agree with such radical ideas as those expressed in Article 27 of the UN charter. There it is stated that governments shall "recognize the right of every child to a standard of living adequate for the child's physical, mental, spiritual, moral, and social development" (UNICEF, 2005, p. 8). Article 27 also makes it clear that governments should assist parents in case of need and help provide material assistance and support programs with regard to nutrition, clothing, and housing.

We actually have several programs to help parents and children, but because they are fragmented, do not cover everyone eligible, and are subject to variability in funding, they end up being not nearly as good nor as serious in intent as those in many other countries. While school critics delight in talking about our inadequate achievement compared to other nations, it seems just as important to talk about other nations' attention to the poor and their mechanisms for helping people get out of poverty. This should be an important indicator for judging one nation's performance against another. If we do that, how will our country fare? It appears that we are a leader among the rich nations of the world in terms of failing to help poor people exit from poverty once they have fallen into it.

I have just pointed out that in the United States the rates of childhood poverty are high, poverty is a racial issue, and those who once get trapped in poverty have a hard time getting out, but what does this mean for us in terms of student achievement? We have research showing connections between poverty and educational achievement. Why do we ignore this research? Instead we look for other causal mechanisms like low expectations of teachers or the quality of the teachers' subject-matter knowledge to explain the relationship.

Why do we put so much of our attention and resources into trying to fix what goes on inside low-performing schools when the causes of low performance may reside outside the school? Is it possible that we might be better off devoting more of our attention and resources than we now do toward helping the families in the communities that are served by those schools?

This may be a successful strategy for solving the problem of low academic performance if it is indeed poverty (along with its associated issues) that prevents most low-income children from doing well. As of now, poverty, race, and ethnicity are inextricably entwined in the United States.

The question remains: can a reduction of poverty improve the achievement of the poor and the schools they are attending?

Putting it bluntly, poverty sucks. Among the poor, it appears that academic talent has been sucked away. Environment is the overwhelming influence on measured IQ among the poor. Unless environments for the most impoverished improve, we will not see the expression of intelligence that is expected.

Another problem arises. We don't know how to improve those environments, because we have not figured out what it is about the environments that is so debilitating. What we do know is that a healthy childhood environment supported by adequate family economics includes a regular supply of nutritious food, stability in feelings of security, quick medical attention when needed, high quality childcare, access to books and exposure to rich language usage in the home, and so forth. School reformers are doing their best and resilient children and the occasionally exemplary school that exist amid poverty should be lauded and supported. However, our focus must remain on the fact that most children in poverty and most schools that serve those children are not doing well.

The simplest way to get a healthier environment in which to raise children is to provide more resources for parents to make those changes for themselves. Despite the shortcomings of many parents at every level of social class, I still believe the proper place to begin solving the problem of achievement among poor families is by making those families less poor. I am not talking about a government giveaway. I seek only employment that can supply families with the income that gives them the dignity and hope needed to survive, allowing them to raise their children well. Is this just a dream, or can we pull together to make it happen?

How would a bit more income per family influence educational achievement? The two answers that immediately spring to mind are health and neighborhood.

There are several health issues that affect the poor. The many medical problems that are related to social class provide obvious and powerful examples of problems affecting school achievement that are remediable with a little extra money. For example, at the simplest level are medical problems such as ear infection and problems associated with vision.

Ear infection is a simple and common childhood affliction, frequently contracted by rich and poor children alike between birth and three years of age. Recurring ear infection in the first three years of life has been related to hearing impairments and thus to language development, and this leads to reading problems in school, which leads to lower testing assessments. Poor children have more untreated cases of ear infection than do those that are financially better off, especially those with medical insurance. The cause of ear infections may not be directly linked to poverty, but its prevalence and lack of treatment in children is quite clearly affected by poverty.

In the final analysis, while ear infection is not a disease of the poor, the characteristics of child rearing and of home environment among the poor of all races and ethnicities leads to more medical problems for the children of the poor. And since low-income families often lack proper medical insurance, they have a much greater chance of having hearing handicaps at the stage of their lives where language is being developed. In just a few years, those handicaps will emerge as reading problems in the classroom.

Ear infection is precisely the kind of problem that is likely not to be much of a factor if the poor were a little richer and in possession of adequate health insurance.

Vision is another simple case of poverty's effects on student behavior outside of the teacher's control. Many of the children tested had some easily correctable vision deficiency, but most cases were not followed up on or corrected. An optometrist working with poor children notes that the mass-screening vision tests that schools typically use rarely assess the ability of children to do close-up work, the work needed to do reading, writing, and arithmetic and engage in computer-mediated learning. What optometrists point out is that a better set of mathematic standards seems less likely to help those students improve in school than direct intervention in their health and welfare. We must ensure that the families of these children earn adequate income and are provided with medical insurance.

The complexity of the medical problems increases when we discuss asthma, which has now reached epidemic proportions among poor children. According to the National Institutes of Health, asthma alone results in 10 million missed school days a year, with many individual children missing 20 to 40 school days a year (National Institutes of Health, 2008).

Asthma is simply preventing millions of all social classes from attending school and studying diligently. Time on task is one of the strongest predictors of learning in schools. When asthma remains untreated, as in the case of the poor, children suffer and learn less.

Another level up in the seriousness of the medical problems that afflict the poor is the effects of lead on mental functioning. Very small amounts of lead can reduce intellectual functioning and diminish the capacity of a child to learn. The damage that lead does is almost always permanent. The good news is that lead poisoning is on the decline. The bad news is that far too many poor children still reside in places that contain lead-painted areas.

Of the millions of children affected in small and big ways by lead poisoning, the majority are poor and mostly children of color. The poor live in older inner-city buildings where lead contamination from paint and lead dust from many other sources are prevalent. But the poor cannot move and cannot afford the paint removal costs since they do not have any income for that.

School buildings may also be an issue. Children attending schools built since 1980 are not being exposed to lead in the paint or in the soil around the schools, while the children in older schools are exposed to toxic levels of this dangerous metal. The students who attend the older schools are usually poor and children of color.

The literature on the symptoms of lead poisoning reminds me of the problems new teachers tell me about when they teach in schools that serve low-income students. A lead-damaged nervous system is associated with a variety of problems, including learning disabilities, attention-deficit hyperactivity disorder (ADHD), increased aggression, lower intelligence, and, for older students, greater likelihood of drug use and criminal behavior (see reviews by Books, 2002 and Rothstein, 2004).

Mercury is a terribly powerful neurotoxin that gets into the air around medical waste–disposal plants and coal-fired power plants. So ask yourself "Who lives in the vicinity of the big urban medical waste facilities or is downwind of a coal-fired power plant?" The answer, of course, is that low-income families, mostly Hispanics and African Americans, are those who live closest to these toxic plants. That is the basis for charges about environmental racism.

Maybe it is even more accurate to call it environmental classism, because those with low incomes feel the brunt of these problems regardless of ethnicity. Again it is clear that low-income children and their parents are getting more lead and more mercury in their systems, suffer more from asthma, and are more prone to untreated ear infection and vision deficiency than their wealthier peers.

What is also important to note is that the symptoms caused by lead and mercury exposure and others mentioned like ADHD, irritability, problems of concentration, and the like, are problems that display degrees of impairment. They are not like pregnancy, where a woman either is or is not. So if the lower classes suffer from these medical issues more than those in the higher classes, then there will be more impairments that are slight, as well as more of those that are more obviously noticeable. These invisible medical problems often translate into misbehavior in school, probably resulting in more lower-income children receiving punishment and having negative school experiences than their healthier middle-class peers.

The set of environmentally caused problems, both small and large, become teacher and school problems that cannot be fixed by administrators and teachers. Yet we have many politicians who worry little about environmental pollution or medical issues among the low-income students, but are quick to blame educators for the poor achievement of some schools. Instead, I believe that more politicians need to turn their attention to the outside-of-school problems that affect inside-of-school academic performance.

There is one more medical problem that is directly related to poverty. Premature births and low birth weight children are much more common problems among the poor. This often leads to a medical belief that brain volume is less in the prematurely born. Premature births and low birth rate are caused by lack of prenatal care, including appropriate diet and vitamins, which happens in low-income families. Lack of medical insurance leads to lack of visits to clinics and doctors. Social class and premature births are also associated with lifestyle problems (drug and alcohol use, vitamin deficiencies) while some are also neighborhood related (waste sites, lead particles). But in any case, the children will still go to public schools five years later.

HOW NEIGHBORHOODS AFFECT THE POOR

Neighborhoods communicate norms for behavior, such as in the case of drugs and alcohol. Low-income neighborhoods reflect socioeconomic characteristics, precisely the kinds of things that make one choose to live in (or not live in) a neighborhood. These include overall unemployment rate, youth unemployment rate, number of single-parent families, percentage of low-earning wage earners, overcrowding, and permanently sick individuals. In the midst of this, school effects are real and powerful. Schools do exert positive influences on the lives of the poor.

Educators know that home circumstances, neighborhood, and school are powerful influences on a student's life, especially secondary students. Neighborhood deprivation shows powerful effects on its own. Tragically, good parents too frequently lose their children to the streets. Families who have enough money to move out of a dysfunctional neighborhood do so. On the other hand, poverty traps people in bad neighborhoods that affect their children separately from the effects of home and school.

Neighborhood affects efforts to influence child development. To combat this we need well-functioning adult role models in our low-income neighborhoods. Positive role models can mean a lot in the lives of poor children. Most low-performing schools serve poor children who live in neglected neighborhoods, and we pay a price for our communal neglect.

We all know that urban segregation of the poor, along with segregation of language minorities and ethnic groups, are reasons for concern. Since the end of World War II, there has been a gradual decline of white middle- and upper-class families in large metropolitan centers. As those families moved to suburbs or small cities, the white middle-class students in the schools in the central cities had to cope with inadequate and decaying housing, weak and failing urban infrastructures, shortages of jobs, and perhaps among the most important of these problems, a critical lack of mentors for urban youth. Without strong positive peer influences and adult mentors, students attending high-poverty schools are not likely to achieve well. We need people who can exert an influence during a child's formative years.

Inner-city youth who are able to attend middle-class schools are exposed to higher expectations and more educational and career options. Many times they have access to knowledge and networks of knowledge unavailable in inner-city schools. These experiences increase their educational and professional opportunities.

Although we have no idea what the microelements of a middle-class culture are, when such a culture is well entrenched in a neighborhood, it is the best insurance that the schools in that neighborhood will have the quality and the student norms of behavior that lead to better academic achievement. The middle-class residentially stable neighborhoods often manifest a collective sense of achievement and that, in turn, determines the ways that youth in these neighborhoods are monitored as they grow up.

On the other hand, neighborhoods that perpetuate the culture of poverty cannot help but have that culture spill over into the schools their children attend. Have our policymakers thought that one way to help the American schools achieve more is to weave low-income housing throughout middle-class areas? (I doubt that it will ever happen.) This would provide more low-income people with access to communities where stability exists and where children have access to a variety of role models. In reality, we are an economically segregated country, a condition perpetuated in various ways by the more affluent and powerful in the nation, so this is not likely to happen.

We could try to harness neighborhood effects on achievement by ensuring that low-income people have access to better-paying jobs so they can make more money and spend more on decent housing. However, in this age of technology one needs an education beyond high school. They can't afford this. The cycle continues. Poverty is what drives families into areas that are not healthy for children and other living things. All these unhealthy things they experience end up, eventually, being dealt with inside the schoolhouse.

I could go on. The rates of hunger among the poor continue to be high for an industrialized nation. Perhaps equally unfortunate is the fact that the neighborhood norms for people who are poor promote nonnutritional foods and diets that lead to medical problems. Anemia, vitamin deficiency, obesity, diabetes, and many other conditions that affect school learning help to keep the academic achievement of poor children lower than it might otherwise be.

The lack of high-quality affordable day care and quality early childhood learning environments is a problem of poverty that also has enormous effects on later schooling. The early childhood educational gap between middle-class and poor children is a fact of life. So why are we not making high-quality early childhood programs available to all our nation's children? Is it economics, or do we just not care?

Income also plays a role in determining the learning opportunities that are available to children during summer months. My experience in the inner-city school system has shown me that children of the lower-income families consistently show greater learning losses over summer than do children of the middle class. The middle-class students get a more nutritious culture and academic diet during the summer than the poor. This results in middle-class children gaining in reading achievement over the summer (due to library programs, parent monitoring, etc.) while lower-class children lose ground. After every summer the gap between the affluent and the poor on the first day of school gets larger and larger.

The effects of smoking, alcohol, and other drugs; lack of adequate dental and medical care; increased residential mobility; fewer positive after-school groups in which to participate; and many other factors all take their toll on the families and children of the poor. While these factors all interact with the quality of the teachers and the schools that poor children attend, these social, educational, medical, and neighborhood problems are also independent of the schools, and thus beyond their control. Poverty severely limits what our schools can be expected to accomplish.

It appears that we have the largest percentage of poor children in the industrialized world, people stay poor longer in the United States than elsewhere in the industrialized world, poverty is negatively related to school achievement, and poverty's effects on our international competitiveness appear to be serious. Poverty has powerful effects on individuals that limit the expression of genetic diversity as well as strongly influencing the health and place of residence in which children are raised. Improvements in the school achievement of students from low-income families will have to come as much from improvements in their outside-of-school lives as from their inside-of-school lives.

There is every reason to suspect that changes in the income of poor families will lead to changes in the school-related behavior and achievement of their children. The simplest way to deal with poverty's effects on achievement is to increase the income of poor people so they are less poor. Rising incomes provide families with dignity and hope, and these in turn promote greater family stability and better child care, all of which help the children succeed better at school and in life.

WHAT DO WE NEED TO DO?

Poverty, through its many connections to other parts of people's lives, is an obstacle that is not easy for most educators to overcome. Poverty in a community almost ensures that many of the children who enter their neighborhood schools cannot maximally profit from the instruction provided there. Finding ways to reduce poverty to improve schooling is a matter of common sense. It takes no great wisdom to realize that families with increasing fortunes have more dignity and hope, and are thus able to take better care of their children, than families in more dire straits, where anxiety and despair are the more common emotional reactions.

Thus, when we push for higher qualifications for the teachers of the poor, as we should, we may also need to push ourselves and others to provide those teachers with children who enter their classrooms healthy and ready to learn. Thirty years ago this was one of our national goals, to be reached by the year 2000. What happened?

There are so many other problems we need to address as well. When we push for more rigorous standards in our schools, we should also push for a raise in the minimum wage, or better yet, for livable wages. If we do not do this, then we will ensure that the vast majority of those meeting the increasingly rigorous requirements for high school graduation will be those students fortunate enough to be born into the right families. If we really want a more egalitarian set of education outcomes, our nation needs a more equalitarian wage structure.

For these same reasons, when we push for more professional development for teachers and mentoring programs for new teachers, we need also to demand that women's wages be set equal to those of men doing comparable work, since it is working women and their children who make up a large percentage of America's poor.

When we push for advanced placement courses or college preparatory curricula for all our nation's students, we must simultaneously demand universal medical coverage for all our children. Only then will all our children have the health that allows them to attend school regularly and learn effectively, instead of missing opportunities to learn due to lack of medical treatment.

When we push for all-day kindergarten or quality early childhood care or detracked schools, we need also to argue for affordable housing throughout our communities so neighborhoods have the possibility of exerting more positive influences on children and people can move from lead- and mercury-polluted areas to those that are less toxic and thus less likely to cause birth defects. This goal requires educators, parents, and other concerned citizens to be in the forefront of the environmental fight. To fight for clean air and water and for less untested chemicals in all our food products is to fight to have more healthy children for our schools to educate. The psychological and financial costs on families and the broader society of students needing special education can be markedly reduced by our demands for a healthier environment.

In my estimation, we will get better public schools by requiring of each other participation in building a more economically equitable society. This is of equal or greater value to our nation's future well-being then a fight over whether phonics is scientifically based, whether standards are rigorous enough, or whether teachers have enough content knowledge.

All I am saying is that I am tired of acting like the schools, all alone, can do what is needed to help more people achieve higher levels of academic performance in our society. We cannot fix inner-city schools without fixing the city in which they are embedded.

The obligation that we educators have accepted—to be accountable to our communities—must become reciprocal. Our communities must also be accountable to those of us who work in the schools, and they can do this by creating social conditions for our nation that allow us to do our jobs well. Accountability is a two-way process. For too long schools have thought of themselves as only agents who must meet the demands of local, state, or federal government. School people need to see communities as agents as well, and therefore hold communities to standards that ensure all our children are accorded the opportunities necessary for success.

It does take a whole village to raise a child, as the old African proverb states, and we actually know a little bit about how to do that. What we seem not to know how to do in modern America is to raise the village to promote communal values that ensure that all our children will prosper. We need to face the fact that our whole society needs to be held as accountable for providing healthy children ready to learn as our schools are for delivering quality instruction. One-way accountability, in which we are always blaming the schools for the faults that we find, is neither just nor likely to solve the problems we want to address.

I am tired, also, of those among us who say the poor are not really so bad off. These critics say our poor today are really much better off than the poor in other countries or compared to the immigrant poor at the turn of the twentieth century. Because of refrigerators, televisions, and automobiles, the poor in America today actually might live better than royalty did in the thirteenth century. What a crazy statement. This fails to capture what poverty is like for poor children.

As a reminder about the reality of poverty, I want to close this chapter with the introduction to *Amazing Grace* by Jonathan Kozol (1995). In doing this I move away from the analytic and quantitative ways to think about poverty and its effects and move to the only way we might actually comprehend the reality of poverty for our young: through the use of narrative.

The Number 6 train from Manhattan to the South Bronx makes nine stops in the 18-minute ride between East 59th Street and Brook Avenue. When you enter the train you are in the seventh richest congressional district in the nation. When you leave, you are in the poorest.

The 600,000 people who live here and the 450,000 people who live in Washington Heights and Harlem, which are separated from the South Bronx by a narrow river, make up one of the largest racially segregated concentrations of poor people in our nation. Brook Avenue, which is the tenth stop on the local lies in the center of Mott Haven, where 48,000 people are the poorest in the South Bronx. Two thirds are Hispanic, one third Black. Thirty-five percent are children.

St. Ann's Church, on St. Ann's Avenue, is three blocks from the subway station. The children who come to this small Episcopal Church for food and comfort, and to play, and the mothers and fathers, who come here for prayer, are said to be the poorest people in New York City. "The poorest of the poor by any standards," says the pastor of St. Ann's.

At the elementary school that serves the neighborhood across the avenue, all of the 800 children qualify for free school lunches. They are classified not only as poor, but also destitute.

In some cities, the public reputation of a ghetto neighborhood bears little connection to the world that you discover when you walk the streets with children and listen to their words. Not so in Mott Haven. By and large, the words of the children in the streets and schools and houses that surround St. Ann's more than justify the grimness in the words of journalists who have described the area.

Crack-cocaine addiction and intravenous use of heroin, which children there call "the needle drug" are woven into the texture of existence in Mott Haven. Nearly 4000 heroin injectors, many of whom are HIV-infected, live there. Virtually every child at St. Ann's knows someone, a relative or neighbor who has died of AIDS, and most children here know many others who are dying now of the disease. One quarter of the women of Mott Haven who are tested in obstetric wards are positive for HIV. Rates of pediatric AIDS, therefore, are very high.

Depression is common among children in Mott Haven. Many cry a great deal but cannot explain exactly why. Fear and anxiety are common. Many cannot sleep.

Asthma is the most common illness among children here. Many have to struggle to take a good deep breath. Some mothers keep oxygen tanks, which children describe as "breathing machines," next to their children's beds.

The houses in which these children live, two thirds of which are owned by the City of New York, are often as squalid as the houses of the poorest children I have visited in rural Mississippi, but there is none of the greenness and the healing sweetness of the Mississippi countryside outside their windows, which are often barred and bolted as protection against thieves.

Some of these houses are freezing in the winter. In dangerously cold weather, the city sometimes distributes electric blankets and space heaters to its tenants. In emergency conditions, if space heaters can't be used because substandard wiring is overloaded, the city's practice is to pass out sleeping bags.

"You just cover up . . . and hope you will wake up the next morning," says a father of four children, one of them an infant one month old, as they prepare to climb into their sleeping bags in hats and coats on a December night.

In humid summer weather, roaches crawl on virtually every surface of the homes in which many of the children live. Rats emerge from holes in bedroom walls, terrorizing infants in their cribs. In the street outside, the restlessness and anger that are present in all seasons frequently intensify under the stress of heat.

In speaking of rates of homicide in New York City neighborhoods, the Times refers to the streets around St. Ann's as "the deadliest blocks" in the "deadliest precinct" of the city. If there is a deadlier place in the United States, I don't know where it is.

Murder is commonplace. In one year alone, 84 people, more than half of whom were 21 or younger, were murdered in the precinct. Ten people were shot dead on a street called Beekman Avenue, viewed by the children living there. On Valentine's Day, three children and three adults were shot dead on the living room floor of an apartment six blocks from the run-down park that serves the area.

The murders continue: three more people were shot in 30 minutes in three unrelated murders in the South Bronx near St. Ann's. A mother was murdered and her baby wounded by a bullet in the stomach while they were standing on a South Bronx street corner, a minister and elderly parishioner were shot outside the front door of their church, another resident was discovered in his bathtub with his head cut off, a man was shot in both eyes gangland style, and a ten-year-old died after being critically wounded in the brain.

Jonathan Kozol concludes his introduction by asking, "What is it really like for children to grow up here? What do they think the world has done to them? Do they believe that they are being shunned or hidden by society? If so, do they wonder why they deserve this? What is it that enables some of them to pray? And when they pray, what do they say to God?"

We don't have a child to waste. We will not be a strong country unless we invest in *all* of our children, especially those steeped in poverty, who really need our help. Our children are essential to America's future.

9

Results Matter

Our lives come to an end the day things don't matter.

—Martin Luther King Jr.

Leo Buscaglia once said, "to each of us, at certain points of our lives, there come opportunities to rearrange our formulas and assumptions, not necessarily to be rid of the old, but more to profit from adding something new." This, to me, is the center of a reform movement. I wrote this book because my thirty-plus years as a teacher and administrator convince me that our schools do need change, serious radical change.

Schools are the most familiar of all civic institutions. You find them in city slums and tree-lined suburbs, Appalachian valleys and mining towns high in the Rockies. They overlook the Atlantic and Pacific oceans and are found in the patchwork of the farms and municipalities of the prairies.

The main article of faith among the Founding Fathers was that a republic could survive only if its citizens were educated. School has continued to shape the core of our national identity.

But achieving a sense of common purpose has never been easy. For over two centuries, public school districts have been political arenas in which citizens have contended with one another. In a society as socially diverse as the United States, controversies about purposes and practices in public schooling are hardly surprising. Such policy debates express both hopes and fears about the nation. When citizens deliberate about the education of the young, they are also deliberating about the shape of the future for the whole nation.

Many say public schools are in deep trouble today. Grim stories appear daily in the media about violence, dropout rates, and low test scores. Beyond such immediate concerns lies uneasiness about purpose, a sense that we have lost our way. As the larger purposes that once gave resonance to public education have become muted, groups that at one time supported public education have become splintered and confused about what to do.

Policy talk about education has always contained plenty of hype and alarm, the hellfire-and-damnation sermon followed by some sort of solution.

Perhaps one reason many Americans feel that we have lost our way in education is that we have forgotten where we have been. Reformers often say that they don't want to look backwards, arguing that amnesia is a virtue when it comes to reinventing education. The problem with that stance is that it is impossible not to look back. Everyone uses some sense of the past in everyday life.

We have lost track of the fact that a child's mind is hungry for knowledge, stimulation, and the excitement learning brings. A child's school should provide these things. The sad thing is that most American schools do not. From kindergarten through high school, our public education system is among the worst in the developed world. For the last fifty years, American schools have operated on the assumption that challenging children academically is unnatural for them, that teachers do not need to know the subjects they teach, and that the learning "process" should be emphasized over the facts being taught. All this is tragically wrong.

Instead of preparing our children for the highly competitive, information-based economy in which we now live, our school policies have severely curtailed their ability and desire to learn.

Mainstream research has shown that if children—all children, not just the privileged—are taught in ways that emphasize hard work, the mastery of basic facts, and rigorous but meaningful testing, their enthusiasm for school will grow, their test scores will rise, and they will become successful citizens in our Information Age global world.

We must remember that different minds learn differently. That is a problem for many children because most schools still cling to a one-size-fits-all educational philosophy. As a result, children struggle to learn due to the fact that their learning patterns do not fit the schools they are in.

Has anyone bothered to consider student profiles? Some students are creative and write imaginatively but do poorly in history because weak memory skills prevent them from retaining facts. Some are weak in sequential ordering and can't follow directions. They may test poorly in math. The problem is not a lack of intelligence, but a learning style that doesn't fit the assignment.

As adults we realize that we cannot be skilled in every area of learning and mastery. Why, then, do we apply tremendous pressure to our children to be good at everything? They are expected to shine in math, reading, writing, spelling, speaking, memorization, comprehension, problem solving, and on and on, while very few adults can do all of this. We need to realize that not every child can do equally well in every type of academic area. We must pay more attention to individual minds. We must maximize children's learning potential. We have the right to differ!

We all know that schools need to change. It is a topic the media promotes. So why is change not happening?

I would like to see the following within schools for all learners.

- Teachers who truly respond to the needs of their students, who base their teaching methods on their understanding of how learning works for each individual.
- Students who are learning about how they learn while they are learning, coupled with gaining insight into who they are.
- Parents who collaborate with schools and join forces with educators to create and sustain schools for all kinds of minds.
- Schools that cultivate diversity as well as make available multiple educational pathways.
- Schools that help students blaze their own trails for creativity, success, and community service.
- Schools that create and maintain an educational plan for each student, and schools in which students can learn at their own natural pace.
- Schools that refuse to label their students.

School occupies more waking hours than kids spend at home, and school life is full of not just studies but human emotion (excitement, fear, envy, love, anger, sexuality, boredom, competitiveness). Students grapple with the textured reality of their lives, devising their own unique strategies to survive and thrive in school. Our job is to help our children find success in school and beyond. How can we not include this in our reform efforts?

All children struggle in life and in school. Learning-disabled children struggle every day with lessons and teaching methods for which their brains are not well suited. School is too much for them on a daily basis. Brilliant children suffer from boredom and loneliness, from feeling misunderstood, from being labeled "nerds." School is not enough for them. The "average" child for whom, presumably, the school experience should be just right, still struggles with mastering new material, with sitting quietly through a long day of classes, with good teachers and bad, with being more popular or less popular with his or her peers. These facts must also be included in our reform efforts.

Whoever summarized school learning as the three basics, "reading, 'riting, and 'rithmetic," grossly underestimated the task that confronts a child at school, and failed to include the most critical coursework of all: the developmental curriculum a child manages in school all day, every day. Moving smoothly through the day, mastering physical skills and factual material, integrating socially into a new classroom, and managing frustration, anger, and disappointment are all part of the developmental agenda of each day. Some students can handle it, others can't.

"My love of learning is still alive. School has not managed to suppress it yet," says a ninth-grader. Will this still be true when he is a senior?

One teacher of tenth-grade language arts was overheard telling his class, "Smart kids are a dime a dozen, personality plus persevering, but you need a lot more than brains to succeed in life." What message is he sending?

I have learned five very important things from students I have worked with, which I believe apply to all students: they are always searching for feelings of success; they come equipped with great "crap detectors"; they do not lie about the nature of their experiences in school; they crave meaningful, reciprocal relationships with adults in the school; and they want to feel useful.

These five characteristics are true of every student, whether he or she is academically gifted or learning disabled, whether he or she comes from a family that values school or not. Teachers sometimes angrily complain that kids don't come to school ready to learn. It is true that not all kids come from homes that give them middle-class, school-friendly values. However, every child draws from these five qualities in the psychological journey of school. Have we considered this in our reform efforts?

Children want to feel successful. This craving is so powerful that you can always count on it. Adults often lose track of this fact and start to believe that kids don't want to succeed in school. Children may confuse us by doing self-destructive things. Because they are scared of being humiliated, they refuse to study for tests. They fail to try. When they become older, they are truant and often drop out.

In our reform efforts, we must build in plans to provide students with meaningful experiences of mastery. The real tragedy occurs when adults forget that kids really want to succeed, when teachers write students off by saying that they don't care, that they don't come to school ready to learn, as if all children know what the academic enterprise requires. It is essential to tap into a child's desire for success. It is there! Remember, an error means that a child needs some help, not a reprimand or ridicule for doing something wrong.

Reform efforts that include classrooms and schools centered on learning and learners lead to intellectually rigorous places that are exciting and humane. Reform efforts should be concerned with honoring individuality, developing potential, and arming kids with an ability to think freely and independently. Good schools best serve learners by allowing good teaching to flourish, reducing bureaucratic demands favoring competition over procedures, nurturing and rewarding professional development, supporting curricula and assessments that are relevant and challenging, and stimulating inside-out change.

Let's consider a reform program that includes the following three objectives. The first objective is enhancing emotional education, cultivating students as emotionally well-rounded human beings and countering the growing decay of school education as shown by bullying, violence, nonattendance, and the breakdown of classroom order. The second is developing a school system that helps children recognize their individuality and gives them diverse choices, shifting the emphasis from uniformity to a diverse, flexible educational system that encourages individuality, thereby cultivating creative human resources. The third is promoting a system in which the school's autonomy is respected, advancing decentralization of educational administration, reinforcing the autonomy of local boards of education, and aiming for independent autonomous school management.

What about combining middle schools and high schools as an option? Some private schools do this already. How about sending superior students directly to the universities, skipping the final year of high school? Some of our nation's seniors are wasting time, taking classes they really don't need to simply "fill in time." Our postsecondary options program tends to allow attendance in college classrooms but still require high school attendance for other classes.

We can design classes that encourage volunteer activities as an aspect of emotional education. For example, schools could require students to engage in two weeks of volunteer activities while in elementary and middle school and one month while in high school.

Reform efforts should lead us to develop schools that focus on helping learners create new knowledge by helping them cope effectively with current laws, rules, and constraints and then help discern when and how and in what manner to defy those rules, laws, and constraints.

Useful learning and growing happen in many ways and in many places. Students learn on field trips, on jobs, on their own, and from each other, as well as from teachers in their classrooms.

Beware that the many school reforms now being advocated are not the very practices that have put American education at risk. Since mistaken ideas have been the root cause of America's educational problems, the ideas must be changed before the problems can be solved.

Reform efforts must lead students to live a life with standards and with questions, living a life in search of meaning. These are not quests. These are realities. Schools need to be for students already living a life, not preparing to live a life. Honor the lives they are presently living. Reclaim the essence of learning.

Human energy is one key to school reform. While money is widely used to symbolize the nutrients schools need to grow, money simply buys time.

Focused human energy is what reform requires. This statement is as true of the first-grade students weaving phonemes into meaningful words as it is of a school district weaving separate projects into an action plan for districtwide reform. Phonemes do not make meaning. The projects do not make change. A school is less an aggregate of things than it is an ongoing interaction among many individuals growing and changing in response to each other. It is the flow of human energy, human intelligence, you might say, that links small initiatives to a larger purpose, bringing flexible shape to the whole. Education's ability to reform its structure while it adapts its functions to fit new purposes depends on a steady flow of human energy.

Large social organizations cannot succeed unless they focus on what they do best. The same is true for schools. What is it that schools and only schools can and must do? They cannot be successful as schools unless nearly all of their pupils gain literacy and numeracy as well as a solid understanding of history, science, literature, and foreign language. They cannot be successful unless they teach children the importance of honesty, personal responsibility, intellectual curiosity, industry, kindness, empathy, and courage.

We keep saying that schools should prepare students to learn new tasks and take charge of their lives, and to use symbolic language and abstract ideas. They need to teach students about the culture and the world in which they live and about cultures that existed long ago. Then why don't we do what we keep saying we must do?

If schools know and affirm what they do well, they can liberate themselves from the fads and panaceas that have often been inflicted on them by pressure groups, legislators, and well-meaning enthusiasts. Schools cannot compete with the visual dramas of television, the Internet, and the movies. But the mass media, random and impersonal as they are, cannot compete with teachers who have the capacity to get to know their students, inspire them, and guide them to maturity.

Schools will not be rendered obsolete by new technologies, because their role as learning institutions has become even more important than in the past. Technology can supplement schooling, but not replace it. Even the most advanced electronic technologies are incapable of turning their worlds of information into mature knowledge, a form of intellectual magic that requires skilled and educated teachers.

To be effective, schools must concentrate on their fundamental mission of teaching and learning, and they must do it for all children. That must be the overarching goal of schools in the twenty-first century. This must be our ultimate challenge.

Reform versus reinvention—what is the answer? Many educators feel the word *failing* is an inaccurate and even damaging label for the issues in public education today. These same educators feel the universally used phrase *educational reform* cannot be a label for the solution.

Our system of public education is more than one hundred and fifty years old. It was "invented" in response to profound changes in our society: the shift from a rural, agrarian economy to one that was rapidly becoming both urban and industrial. At the same time, America was opening its doors to large numbers of immigrants from around the world. We needed more than an unregulated system of one-room schoolhouses. We needed an assembly-line form of education that would standardize the delivery of basic skills, the three r's, to large numbers of students.

When the public speaks about reform today, they are at least as concerned about values as they are about academics. They are concerned about a set of traits they call life skills. They are concerned about an apparent lack of a work ethic. Today's youth appear less motivated by traditional incentives than previous generations were.

Beneath the broad umbrella of what is called educational reform we find that different groups have specific concerns. However, all have, in some way, to do with the impact of change in our society and on the young. Yes, adults want all students to master the basics, but they are equally concerned about students' values and motivation for work and learning. Many realize that in today's economy the level and quality of one's education is more important than ever and so are committed to providing equal educational opportunities for *all* students.

What more and more Americans will soon come to discover is that current educational reform efforts do not address many of their deepest concerns about our schools. Because of the increased emphasis on passing high-stakes tests, schools do not have the time to teach anything else other than what is in the tests. Nor is there time to worry about the increasing minority dropout rate or the apparent apathy of young people, made worse by all the emphasis on tests. Worst of all, the tests tell us very little about the qualities of mind and heart that matter most for success and happiness in adult life.

Our challenge is in dealing with the future. The struggle is between those who believe that the best way to deal with change is to cling to remnants of the past and those who eagerly embrace the future. We must face the new challenges that change brings to education while strengthening those values and institutions that are most important to us.

We must make sure that *all* students have both the skills and values they need for work and citizenship in a rapidly changing world. We must motivate *all* students to want to achieve higher standards, both intellectually and morally, despite the growing influence of an amoral popular culture that encourages consumption, not creation.

We must provide a framework and some starting points while we consider reforming or reinventing American public education. I believe we must together consider the following.

- What should *all* high school graduates know and be able to do? What does it mean to be an educated adult in America today?
- What about testing and assessment?
- How do we hold students, teachers, and schools accountable?
- How do we motivate *all* students to want to achieve at higher levels in a world that is more demanding and confusing than ever?
- What should schools of the future look like? And how do we motivate educators and other stakeholders to work together to create them?
- How can we share responsibility among politicians, business and community leaders, citizens, educators, and parents in helping to improve our schools?

Living in a world of rapid change, we need to understand more deeply what students need to know and be able to do, as well as what kinds of schools will be most helpful to them. These questions will help us consider how a changing world is shaping today's young people and their future.

No uniform human "product" will ever flow from the pipelines of education. Instead, schools are producing a diversified assortment of human beings. We hope that education intensifies personal strengths and affinities sufficiently while providing broad exposure to the diverse realms of knowledge and skills.

When you think about it, schools are a lot like airport hubs. Student passengers arrive from many different backgrounds and take off for widely divergent destinations. Their takeoffs into adulthood will demand different flight plans. Fortified with this understanding of student learning, we can affirm an educational reform plan that values, respects, and preserves all kinds of minds, beginning during early childhood and continuing through our entire lives.

The public needs to break out of its lethargy and become knowledgeable about education, much as they are about business and home buying. The public must be in a position to challenge the public educational system, the so-called educational establishment (tight groups of teachers, principals, superintendents, professors of education, and counsels to the states' commissioners of education).

The usual remedies, from federal aid to smaller class sizes, have done nothing to alleviate these problems because they make no attempt to challenge the educational establishment's control.

We can't reform our schools unless we stop being afraid of change. We will never be successful in our reform efforts unless we run our schools like businesses, make the media our partners, empower our teachers to teach, and hold our educators accountable. We must make school more exciting than the streets.

So what shall we make of all this? Some of the school reform efforts are thinly disguised elitist attempts to get rid of public education, to protect the privilege such individuals have already bestowed on their children. After all, the greater the disparities in education, the greater the assurance that the privileged have someone to mow their lawns, to wait at their tables, and to care for their children. The reforms they offer—higher standards, a tougher curriculum, and more tests, with no increase in spending—will ensure that the children of New Trier High School, near Chicago; and the children of Princeton, New Jersey; and the children of Manhasset, New York, will succeed even more than they do today. The children of PS 79 in the Bronx, New York, will fail at even greater rates than they do today. Children at PS 79 and similar schools in Los Angeles, California; Camden, New Jersey; Detroit, Michigan; and San Antonio, Texas, schools described so poignantly by Jonathan Kozol, do not have textbooks for their students, are forced to hold some of their classes in closets, teach word-processing skills without computers, teach science classes without laboratories, and conduct physical education and art classes without proper equipment. These are schools that cannot regulate heating or cooling or keep out the rain. Their teachers are often those rejected by the wealthier suburbs, and large percentages of their classes are taught by uncertified people.

Reforms of the kind being proposed will often exacerbate the differences between the have and the have-not school districts. The haves are already doing quite well. Those children of privilege are attending decent schools, achieving well, scoring well on standardized tests, graduating high school, and going to college. They are the smartest and healthiest generation America has ever produced. There really is not much to reform for these kids, since their schools are not failing, at least by the traditional measures we use to assess such things. On the other hand, schools that are to break the mold, that will address the social issues causing parts of our nation's school system to be in ruins, are still fighting for survival.

We need to look at goals that will address the real failures of our schools more directly. First, let us agree with our educators that all children should come to school ready to learn. Let us therefore provide high-quality day care and preschool to all American children and ensure that they and their families have the finest health care in the world. This is how we can ensure that they will come to school ready to profit.

Second, let us choose to have safe schools. But let us go on to guarantee every child a school where plumbing works, where toilet paper and supplies are available, where heating and cooling systems are operational, where the rain does not run into the school building, and where the plaster is not falling. Let us guarantee each child access to current textbooks, computers, and science laboratories and provide children who are eligible with the bilingual education to which they are legally entitled. Maybe we could just guarantee that every child in America shall have a certified teacher who knows his or her name and family.

Third, we should be number one in the world in the percentage of eighteen-year-olds that are politically and socially involved. Far more important than our mathematics and our science scores is the involvement of the next generation in maintaining our democracy and helping those within it that need assistance: the young, the ill, the old, the handicapped, the illiterate, the hungry, and the homeless. Schools that cannot turn out politically active and socially helpful citizens should be identified and their rates of failure announced in the media.

Fourth, we should equalize the funding for schooling so that schools in one part of the state or even within a district cannot spend twice or three times more per child per year than other schools in the state.

We must be very careful that the campaign to discredit the American school system and to blame it for the ills of our nation does not lead to making the wrong decisions about what to fix. Greater school improvement will come from providing poor people with jobs that pay enough to allow them to live with dignity than from all the fooling around we can do with curriculum and instruction or with standards and tests. Children who are poor, unhealthy, and from families and neighborhoods that are dysfunctional do not do well in schools. Educators cannot work miracles. Children from families that have some hope, some income, and some health care have a chance.

Educators must now speak up. It is time for us to inform the politicians and business leaders of America that we cannot solve all the problems that they are creating. We will no longer take blame for their actions. All of us in this nation must find ways to help each family live with dignity so those families can give their children hope. Education is irrelevant to those without hope and succeeds remarkably well for those who have it.

The drive to learn is strong. Learning is at once deeply personal and inherently social. It connects us to knowledge in the abstract and to each other. Throughout our lives, as we move from setting to setting, we encounter novelty and new challenges, small and large. If we are ready for them, living and learning become inseparable.

The challenges facing American schools are complex and often difficult to solve. Still, the mood is optimistic. Excellent teachers, willing businesspeople, enthusiastic parents, and talented students are already involved in the quest for reform. However, our schools will not flourish and our students will not become educated unless the entire nation recognizes and acts to seek improvement and advocate for change. The crisis is upon us. We have no choice but to reform our schools. Unless we do, our prospects are dim: our nation is weakened, our democracy diminished, and our future limited. Life isn't about waiting for the storm to pass; it's about learning to dance in the rain.

I would like to conclude with two quotes for you to ponder.

Thomas Jefferson said that the future of a democracy depends on the education of its people. Today, education needs our support. Will we give all children what they need to succeed, or stand by and see their opportunities limited? The choice we make will determine the future of our children and our nation.

Joseph Addison, an English essayist and poet, wrote in 1711, "Education is a companion which no misfortune can depress, no crime can destroy, no enemy can alienate, no despotism can enslave. Education is at home a friend, abroad an introduction, in solitude a solace, in society an ornament. Education chastens vice, it guides virtue, it gives at once grace and government to genius. Without education, what is man? A splendid slave, a reasoning savage" (Bernard and Mondale, 2001, p. 108).

Indeed, we are still a nation at risk, but it is our children and their future that are more at risk than our economy or national security. Students are at risk of graduating without the skills needed today for work, lifelong learning, citizenship, and personal growth and health. They are at risk of leaving school without once experiencing the joy of learning or connecting with a caring adult. They are at risk because their lives are all too often lacking in purpose or direction, meaning and hope. And with so many of our children at risk in these ways, our future as a nation is also at risk. These children are our future. We have no other.

Our children are counting on us.

References

Beals, M. P. (1994). *Warriors Don't Cry: A Searing Memoir of the Battle to Integrate Little Rock Central High.* New York: Pocket Books.

Berliner, D. (2006). "Telling the Stories." *Educational Psychologist,* 42(2), pp. 50–63. Lawrence Earlbaum Associates, Inc.

Bernard, S. and Mondale, S. (2001). *School: The Story of American Public Education.* Boston, MA: Beacon Press.

Blankinship, D. G. (2006, December 2). "Politicians Weigh High Standards against Angry Parents." Associated Press. *The Tacoma News Tribune.* http://www.thenews tribune.com/news/education/story/6263818p-5466370c.html.

Books, S. (2002). *Poverty and Environmentally Induced Damage to Children.* New York: Teachers College Press.

Carnegie Foundation for the Advancement of Teaching. (2004). *School Choice.* Princeton, NJ. (ED 352 727).

Comer, J. (1988). "Educating Poor Minority Children." *Scientific America,* 259(5), pp. 42–48.

Cremin, L. (1961). *The Transformation of the School.* New York: Knopf.

Douglass, H. (1949, February–March). "The New Movement for Life Adjustment." *Secondary Education,* pp. 1–3.

Education Week. (2006, June 11). "2006 Annual Survey."

Fullan, M. (2003). *Change Forces: Probing the Depths of Educational Reform.* London: The Falmer Press.

Goodlad, J. (1995, March). "A Portrait of John Goodlad." *Educational Leadership,* 52(6), pp. 5–12.

Greene, J. (2006, June 27). "High School Drop-out Rates Rise." Transcript: PBS Online News Hour. http://www.pbs.org/newshour/bb/education/jan-june06/dropout-06_27.html.

Hirsch, E. D. Jr. (1995). *Core Knowledge Sequence.* Charlottesville, VA: Core Knowledge Foundation.

——— (1996). *The Schools We Need*. New York: Doubleday.

Ipka, F. (2008). "Growing School Reform." *NASSP Bulletin*, 106(606), pp. 8–9.

Kidder, T. (1989). *Among School Children*. Boston, MA: Houghton-Mifflin.

Kozol, J. (1995). *Amazing Grace: The Lives of Children and the Conscience of a Nation*. New York: Crown Press.

National Commission of Excellence in Education. (1983). *A Nation at Risk*. Washington, DC: U.S. Department of Education. www.ed.gov/pubs/Nation at Risk/risk.html.

National Institute of Health. (2008). "Children's Asthma in America." Department of Health and Human Services. Bethesda, MD: Government Press.

Ravitch, D. (2000). *Left Back: A Century of Failed School Reforms*. New York: Simon & Schuster.

Rothstein, R. (2004). *Class and Schools: Using Social, Economic, and Educational Reform to Close the Black-White Achievement Gap*. Washington, DC: Economic Policy Institute.

Sizer, T. R. (1992). *Horace's School: Redesigning the American High School*. New York: Houghton-Mifflin.

Slaven, R. and Madden, N. (2001). *One Million Children: Success for All*. Thousand Oaks, CA: Corwin Press.

Tayack, D. and Hansot, E. (1982). *Managers of Virtue: Public School Leadership in America*. New York: Basic Books.

Toppo, G. (2006, June 20). "Big-city Schools Struggle with Graduation Rates." *USA Today*. http://www.usatoday.com/news/education/2006-06-20-dropout-rates_x.html.

UNICEF. (2005). "Child Poverty in Rich Countries." Innocente Report Card no. 6. Florence, Italy: UNICEF Innocente Research Center. Retrieved October 8, 2008, from www.UNICEF.org/irc and www.UNICEF-irc.org.

Webster's New World Dictionary. (2005). New York: Houghton-Mifflin.

Witte, J. (2004, December). *Milwaukee Parental Choice Program*. Madison, WI: University of Wisconsin Institute of Public Affairs.

About the Author

Darlene Leiding is an expert in the realm of charter schools and alternative education, and has used her experience to create an elementary and high school alternative program operating within the Minneapolis Public Schools contracted alternative system. She has currently accepted a position with the administrative team at High School for the Recording Arts, located in St. Paul, Minnesota. She is also the author of four educational books for Rowman & Littlefield Education.